Published by:

Pietas Publications
Waynesboro, Virginia, USA
web: www.jasperburns.com
email: pietas@jasperburns.com

A Lady in Jamaica

1879

By Martha Jefferson Trice

Edited by Jasper Burns

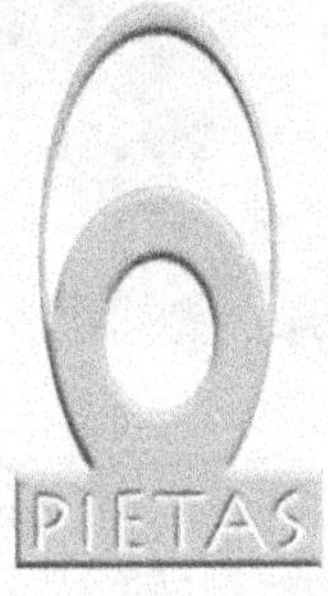

Martha Jefferson Trice in New York City after her travels in Jamaica.
Photo taken by W. Kurtz, 23rd Street and Broadway East, July 16, 1879.

Preface

On July 16, 1879, a frail but lovely young woman from Virginia stepped in front of a camera at W. Kurtz's studio in Madison Square, New York City for a full length portrait. The flash powder exploded and the picture was taken. Her expression was sweet but somewhat melancholy, perhaps because she had just completed a long sea voyage from Jamaica; perhaps because she was homesick and ill and not used to big cities. She couldn't have known that in just one year and eight days she would die of typhoid fever at the age of 25.

Martha Jefferson Trice (May 6, 1855-July 24, 1880) was named for her maternal grandmother Martha Jefferson Terrell Minor (1793-1860) who was named for her maternal grandmother Martha Jefferson Carr (1746-1811) - the sister of Thomas Jefferson. Their family was socially prominent and well-connected, but the Civil War and the early demise of the men of their branch of the family for five consecutive generations had left them with little more than refinement and education.

However, that education was among the best available to a young woman in Virginia at the time. Martha's great grandmother Lucy Carr Terrell had grown up at Monticello under the tutelage of her uncle, the president and polymath. Lucy's daughter Martha was a teacher and passed on the family's intellectual tradition to her daughter and granddaughters. Martha Trice herself was a teacher, specializing in English and French, as well as a published poet. Literature was her passion, and her eye for beauty and detail, both in nature and in the written word, make her Jamaican journal vivid and moving as well as historically interesting.

Martha's upbringing had been genteel and reasonably comfortable, though severely disrupted by the Civil War and the death of her father when she was not quite 9. He died as the result of a chill that overtook him after venturing forth in foul weather to sign up for military service at the age of 48. Robert Nelson Trice was remembered as "a man of great intelligence, a most successful farmer, and highly esteemed for his happy, genial disposition and cultivated powers."

After her husband's death in 1864, Martha's mother Lucy Jane Minor Trice (1822-1876) struggled to cope with her loss and the turmoil that attended the war's end while raising five children (four girls and one boy) aged three to thirteen. The eldest child, a girl named Mary Jane, died only two months after her father.

Lucy Jane Trice was a gifted, highly emotional, and very literary woman. She had been quite sickly in her youth and in her mid-thirties began having the strokes that would eventually kill her. In her late teens she wrote:

"Oh Fame, had I but fame, I could die happy; or I could bear my living death with resignation. Can it be that these burning aspirations after genius, this yearning desire for fame shall forever remain unsatisfied? Oh! To leave a name to be handed down to posterity, to be immortalized as Shakespeare or Scott, would be perfect happiness."

After the death of her husband, Mrs. Trice divided her time between Charlottesville and Mychunk, the family farm east of town near Keswick. The cultural atmosphere in this home during Martha's childhood was described by Edward C. Mead in his book, *Historic Homes of the Southwest Mountains of Virginia*:

The Machunk Farm has been frequently the scene of much refined gayety. The literary tastes of Mrs. Trice and her daughters were of the highest type, which gave them delight in entertaining those of similar dispositions. Here the charm of bright classic minds, combined with love of poetry, song, and music, made this delightful home one never to be forgotten.

A diary entry by an 11 year-old visitor to Mychunk in 1871 shows that classic minds were also capable of silliness:

Saturday was the first day of April and Cousin Margaret Trice fooled Cousin Martha. She took a cup and filled it half full of salt and the other half was coffee. Cousin Martha stirred it up and took a big spoonful and what a face she did make!

Mrs. Trice died in 1876, leaving her remaining four children to fend largely for themselves, though they could rely on guidance and support from many close relatives and friends. At the time of their mother's death, Martha was not quite 21, her older sister Margaret Thurston Trice was 22, her younger sister Lucy Lee Trice 19, and their brother Dabney Minor Trice 15.

The young Trices carried on at Mychunk (also spelled Machunk and Mechunk). Letters from this period reveal that money was in short supply, however. While young Dabney struggled to make the farm profitable, his two oldest sisters took in young girls as boarding students. In late 1878, Martha came very close to accepting a position as teacher in Ohio, though this fell through at the last moment. Despite these financial straits, the Trice sisters managed to travel – Martha to Jamaica in 1879 and her sister Lucy also to Jamaica in 1879-1880 and to Europe in 1884. These trips were at least partly paid for by prosperous relatives – Martha's trip seems to have been a gift from her hosts.

The Jamaica trips were visits with the Evans family, close friends and former neighbors of the Trices. Mrs. Sophia Evans (1811-1885) lived there with her daughter Sophy, who was five years older than Martha, and her son St. George, who had romantic intentions toward Martha that were not reciprocated.

When Martha returned to Virginia in July of 1879, she was accompanied by Sophy Evans, who spent several weeks at Mychunk before sailing back to Jamaica with Martha's sister Lucy in October. Two months later, on December 10, 1879, Sophy married William Panton Forbes at Spring Garden, Jamaica with Lucy Trice in attendance.

A major reason for Martha's trip to Jamaica was the hope that her health would improve with the change of climate. Indeed, she was described as stronger than she had been after her return in July, but still very weak. Her sister Margaret's letter to a close relative in early August is revealing:

[The doctor} says she must keep perfectly quiet – must not ride, drive, or go up and down steps, must paint her stomach with iodine, use carbolic acid, take a strong tonic, etc., etc. By doing all these things he thinks she may escape another abscess & in about six weeks be nearly well.

Unfortunately, whatever temporary improvement Martha experienced would not last for long. She suffered from various attacks in early 1880, requiring treatments with bromide, morphine, chloral, quinine, arsenic, and strychnine. Then, in early July - just a few weeks after her sister Lucy's return from Jamaica, typhoid fever hit the neighborhood of Mychunk and took the lives of both Martha (July 24) and her sister Margaret (July 30), and very nearly that of her brother Dabney as well.

Martha's and Margaret's epitaph, divided between their gravestones, side by side in Maplewood Cemetery, Charlottesville, Virginia, is sweet and simple: *They were lovely and pleasant in their lives...and in their death they were not divided.*

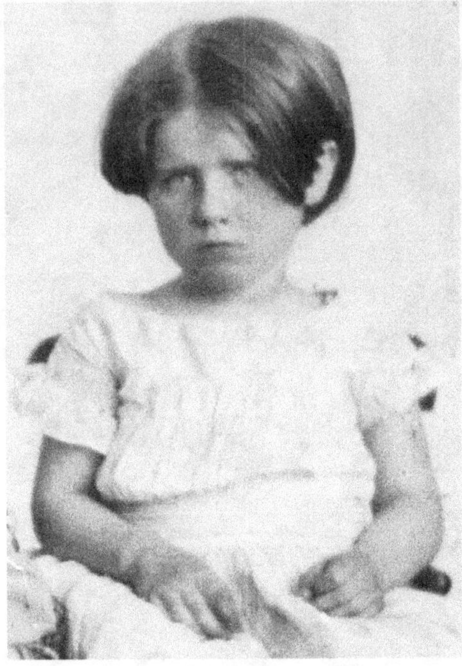

Martha, aged two, 1857

Martha Jefferson Trice, circa 1878

My Journal

Commenced Jan. 30th 1879.

I must go back a few days in the beginning of my record and start from the time I left my dear sisters at Keswick to pay the visit to Jamaica which I have just begun. When I got on the train, there were a great many men on board and but two girls, so of course I gave myself up to my own reflections until we reached Washington. There I changed into a Pullman's palace car, which certainly well-deserved its name for it was exceedingly handsome. It was furnished throughout with carved and gilded walnut and crimson velvet, and all the appointments for washing were white marble and plate. There I passed quite a comfortable night as the Northern railway is so very much smoother than the one from Ch'ville to Washington. The train reached New York at 6.45, where Cousin Waller met me and we crossed by the steam ferry.

On our way up to Lexington Avenue we passed the ruins of a large clothing establishment which had been burned a few days before. It had occupied a whole block and dozens of men were busy picking out hundreds of suits, some scorched, and some entirely burnt. I also saw the new Catholic church that is going up [St. Patrick's]. It will be the handsomest in America. It is white marble with a great deal of fretwork and carving.

Kate gave me a very warm reception and I stayed quietly with her all day. She was very anxious for me to go out and see the city but I was dreadfully tired and suffering a good deal from the unusual exertion. Cousin Waller [Waller Holladay (1840-1907)] showed me something very curious that night. It was a manuscript in Syriac. The letters were very curiously formed and looked like hieroglyphics but what was most strange, all the vowels were little red dots between the lines.

We got up very early this morning to get to the steamer, and drove down in a carriage. We came through 5th Ave. to see some of the handsome buildings and amongst others was A. T. Stewart's house. His body has just been recovered. [A. T. Stewart was an extremely wealthy merchant – one of the 20 richest men of all time. After his death, his body was stolen and held for ransom.] The great Central Depot was one of the largest buildings I ever saw. Indeed the glimpse I got of

New York was quite tantalizing, it made me want to see more of it so much.

Grand Central Depot, New York City, 1880

And now at last I come to my getting on board the *Etna*. Cousin Waller introduced me to the captain, who was very cordial, said he would take the very best care of me and gave me a seat just beside him at table. Then I was shown to my cabin. I am entirely alone and monarch of all I survey, but my territory is quite limited. Indeed to tell the truth, I am quite disappointed in my cabin. It is about half as large as our little dressing room and has four berths, so there is not more than 3 feet of width, most of which is occupied by my trunk and valise, so I will have to occupy my berth if I stay in there much. The captain advises however that I shall stay on deck as much as possible to prevent the dreaded *"mal de mer."*

I have been on deck for an hour or two watching the beach of Long Island as it gradually disappeared from view, and talking to the captain. He is a nice, good looking bronzed face man, who is just as kind and pleasant as he can be. He is an Englishman and is very intelligent. We have had a long chat about Dickens, who he adores, and all of whose works he has at his finger ends. When he was a little boy nine years old he was a proof reader at Bradbury and Evans, who were Dickens' publishers, and he was sent every Friday evening to D.'s house to get the manuscript. He said he wrote just like Count Fosco in "Woman in White" did his confession, and by the way did you know Dickens helped Wilkie Collins to write that book. You remember how he wrote on little strips and threw them on the floor and Dickens wrote just that way. He said he was exceedingly dilatory and always kept him waiting, but was very kind. The captain's name is Ferguson. The ship is not a nice one at all, it is very dirty and they give you a very limited supply of water.

The dinner bell broke short my writing, and after dinner which was at 5 we all went up stairs to the little deck room, which is about as large as the little room off the Sampson's dining room, and chatted until eleven when we went to bed.

Now I must tell you about the passengers. The nicest are two Jews, one a very handsome man who sits next me at table and is very attentive. He is about 50, very tall and well formed with the exception of his hands. He was born with only 3 fingers on his left hand and no right hand at all. The arm only dwindles to a point. He cuts up his food with perfect ease and don't seem to mind it at all. He is a commission merchant named Lazarus, of the great London firm of that name, and is enormously wealthy. He is a great traveller. I forget the name of the other Jew, though the captain told it me. He is a native of Jamaica and a grower of bitter wood, quassia, china wood, etc. Then there is a young Englishman just like Tommy Macon in appearance, voice and all. He is just from Nassau and talks of it a great deal.

Then come a group who are travelling together, a young, fair Frenchman, and two ladies, one young, florid, and just now very seasick, and the other about 35, looking just like a dried monkey. She cannot speak one word of English, and the others only talk it in a very broken manner, which is scarcely intelligible. They have a tiny white Spanish poodle covered with blue ribbons, which the man told us was "ver, ver hard". We suggested "rare," "Oui, oui, rar', ver' rar' he wort, two hunder and feefty dollare."

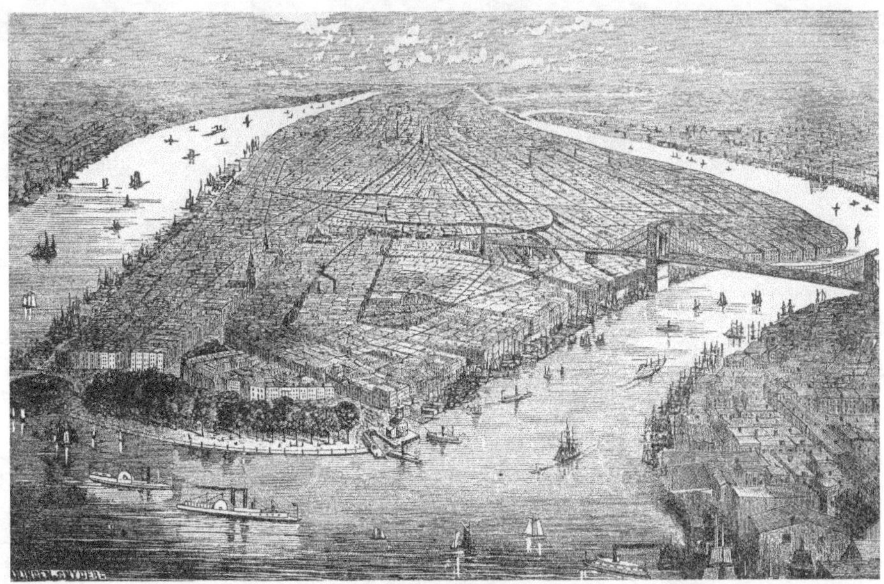

New York City in the 1880s

Martha's sisters and brother.
Top left: Margaret Thurston Trice (1853-1880), ca. 1878,
Top right: Lucy Lee Trice (1857-1897),
photo taken in Kingston, Jamaica, February 26, 1880,
Bottom: Dabney Minor Trice (1860-1915, ca. 1878

Then there is another young man, very young and good looking with beautiful brown eyes, who I have rather a suspicion belongs to the ship's company. He saw me looking very disconsolate on deck yesterday evening, and came up and tried to entertain me, for which I was very grateful, for I have never felt so lonely and desolate, such an atom in the immensity of God's creations as since I have been at sea. Everything is so vast, and one feels so utterly insignificant.

Three lovely white seagulls followed us yesterday for 20 or 30 miles, never settling on anything. I cannot realize how their wings can be so strong as they are not very large. The sea is very smooth, the Captain says, but the constant motion and the noise of the engine makes my head swim very much. They all compliment me very much on being a good sailor, as I have not been sick yet, but it will not do to boast. I feel as if I would willingly give up my entire trip to Jamaica just for one glimpse of my darlings at home. It all came over me with a rush this morning when I opened my bible and Dab's and Margie's pictures dropped out [her brother Dabney and sister Margaret. I could hardly bear to look at them, yet I would give anything to have my darling little Luly's [her sister Lucy Lee] with me, it would be such a comfort to me.

I am writing in the little deck cabin, for my cabin down stairs is such a horrid little hole I avoid it as much as possible. The smells are very unpleasant below and well calculated to make one sick. We are about passing Virginia now and my dear, dear home is as plainly in my mind's eye as if I really saw it. I believe I must have left my heart behind me there, for I can think of nothing else.

We lost sight of land yesterday evening and will not see it again before Tuesday, if it pleases God to spare us. I cannot feel very uneasy for I know I am just as safely in the hollow of his hand here as on land. I was quite shocked when I opened my trunk to find how it had been abused on the journey to New York. The straps and handles were broken half in two and the entire bottom of the tray out, and my things in a nice state of confusion. They must have been extremely careless.

Feb. 3rd Monday.

I have not been able to write any since Friday morning, as the dreaded enemy the terrible *mal de mer* came upon me and I was very sick for a day and night. Since then, though I have been so wretchedly weak as scarcely to be able to lift my hand to my head, still I have been comparatively free from seasickness. The captain compliments me very much on being a good sailor. Yet he says it is because I am so ill I have not enough stamina to be seasick. I believe he thinks me far gone in consumption. He is a dark, gray-bearded Englishman named Ferguson and no father could be kinder to me than he is. He even sees to having my chicken and beef tea made for me himself, and never leaves me for over ten minutes from the time I come up early in the morning until I go below at eleven at night when he helps me down the companion ladder and carries my pillows.

Although I have not been very seasick, still I have been quite ill enough to be extremely uneasy about myself, as another abscess has formed and has caused me a great deal of suffering lately. I am entirely alone as regards female society as the only two ladies on board besides myself are a Countess Patrizzio and another woman who she calls Marie. They are both common actresses and the Captain says bold, bad women and told me to take no notice of them and to come to him if they annoyed me. We only exchange the common civilities. I handed the Countess my cologne the other day when she was very sick, and she said "Ah! tank you, tank you, I was veri stupide not to brieng mee own."

Then there is the German Jew of New York, Mr. Weinshank, who has been very sick and he constantly comes in and informs us, "I feels very ill, bud I have joost paid my tribute to de sea and now I feels mooch bedder." My brown eyed youth turns out to be the Captain's clerk, he seems very clever and polite, but is kept very busy.

The sea has been so rough since Friday that we have had to keep all the ports closed even in the little deck cabin upstairs. The sea was washing over the decks all day yesterday, and the sheets were so wet last night I had to sleep between the blankets. The day I was worst, Sat., it rained hard all day and the sea was very rough, and the kind good captain would not leave me shut up with the disreputable foreigners, so he sat by me and talked to me or read me little bits out of the newspapers, and whenever he had to go, he always sent the stewardess up to sit with me. Last night the sea was so high it washed into the little deck room, quite flooding it, and drenching us.

We have been passing through seaweed or rather gulfweed since yesterday morning and this morning the captain made a tiny wire grappling iron and caught me some. I shall keep it for the dear ones at home. I have never been so homesick in my life as since I have been at sea, every minute of every hour the dear, dear faces are before me, and I do so yearn for them. Yesterday I lay and read the service and thought of them all day long. If I ever return to them God knows I shall never leave them again.

One never feels so fully the dependence on a Divine will as on the great waste of waters. You can do nothing, only trust to a Father's care, and last night even though there was quite a gale and the captain had just been showing me how to put on the life preserver, I went below and slept as peacefully as on land. That is to say I slept a little for I have been almost entirely sleepless since I have been on board.

Kingston Harbor, 1870. The steamship in the center is approximately the size of the Etna.

Tomorrow when it gets smoother the Captain is going to show me over the ship. Everybody is particularly kind to me, even the rough common sailors come several times a day to ask how I am, and the passengers are always offering me apples, oranges, etc. I am worse than I have been since Xmas, and I sometimes fear I shall never be strong and well again, for to put my feet down even one moment brings on terrible pain, and the stairs loom before me like a mountain range.

We are in the region of flying fish now, I hope I may see one. We hope to see land this evening, San Salvador. We have not seen any since we left Long Island. The first rough weather was off Cape Hatteras, and then it became more and more rough as we passed the Gulfstream. We are going very fast with a Northerly wind, it is the quickest trip the Captain has ever made, he smiled at me when I said it was rough and said, "Oh it is a fine Northerly breeze and only a bit roughish," but last night he acknowledged it was rougher than usual at this latitude.

Today, however, a great change, much warmer and the sea a dark deep blue, a "regular navy blue." The day we left New York, it was quite black because it was not very deep. The next day it grew green and now is deep blue, because, as the captain says, there is no bottom to it. I quote the captain constantly because I do not talk to anyone else much and he is always telling me various things to entertain me. I am afraid he will quite spoil me by his kindness. He told me last night, if I wished I might stay up here in the little deck room instead of going down to the cabin, though it is positively against the rules of the ship and he would get the steward to watch, lest I should be frightened, but of course I could not have the poor man standing out in the drenching spray all night so I went down below.

The gulfweed is just like mistletoe when it is first fished up, but very soon loses its freshness and dries up. The captain has been telling me a great many stories about his having been wrecked. The first time was in the Gulf of St. Lawrence and before the lifeboat got to them and took them off, seven of the men were frozen to death. He was frozen to the rigging and the ice and snow were two inches thick on him. An old Canadian woman cut all the ends of his fingers and let out the black blood. They would have rotted off in another hour.

Then another time he was shipwrecked in the Gulfstream and he told of it while we were being tossed about in it, pleasant wasn't it?). The ship was caught in a hurricane and the boats went first so they had nothing to save themselves with, but the gale was tremendous all night, and in the morning the ship broke right in half and they were left on the waters, seventeen men with only bits of ladders etc. to float with and no vessel in sight. But in only 3 hours an Italian brig came and picked them up and took them on to Gibraltar. He said they nearly starved on the voyage however as the Italians had only macaroni and very little of that.

He told me too that as we had always heard Dickens represented his own life in writing David Copperfield, but what I did not know before that Dickens beginning in life was even humbler than David's as he corked and labeled wine bottles and Dickens only blacking bottles. Then his life as a reporter for Parliament was identical with David's.

I am getting so very tired I must stop writing now as it is very troublesome to do it at all, as the ship is still rolling a good deal, though nothing to compare with yesterday. I would give up my whole journey with all its anticipations just to be once again with my darlings. Oh! if we were only bound for New York instead of Jamaica. The only place for sick people is at home. And to think of my leaving my dear, dear home for a strange country. I ought never to have done it for "My heart's in Virginia wherever I go." Nobody ever had dearer ties than I have.

Tuesday, Feb. 4th

Yesterday the captain was eating some oysters, when he found a good-sized pearl in one of them, rather dark, but quite as large as the head of a large darning needle. Last night it was beautiful, the waves glittered and glanced like liquid silver in the moonlight and what added very much to our pleasure, all of the stewards and waiters went to one side of the deck and sang a number of songs. They were all familiar ones, "Then you'll remember me, Katy Wells, Speak to me speak," etc. and as they kept perfect time it was very sweet indeed.

Last night I went down to dinner for the first time since the day I came on board, not from seasickness but I have been so terribly weak that I have only been able to get up in the morning and down again at night and only then with assistance. Well, when I went down, to my surprise I was greeted with quite an ovation, everybody seemed so glad to see me and wanted me to drink wine with them. Indeed Mr. Lazarus my next neighbor and the captain quite worry themselves whether I eat or not. Mr. L. has a supply of fine oysters and oranges on board and he proffers them to me at all hours, and yesterday the captain asked me to order the dinner today and to have any delicacy I wished made at any time. Imagine it, when I have everything I want, and more too as somehow my appetite I was so proud of before I left Va. has unaccountably vanished, I think on account of this abscess, but you have no idea how grateful I am for all this kindness from these old men and how it touches me.

I fear my journal will seem very egotistical to my darlings if they ever see it but I see nothing but sea and sky. Last night I sat up very late to see the Bird Rock Lighthouse on one of the Bahamas, or more correctly on a rock four miles from one of them. I walked with the captain to the prow of the vessel to see it. It revolves once in a minute and a half and is very brilliant. We passed another at five this morning. This morning it was so warm and bright I passed an hour or two lying on the aft hatch under the awning and reading *Zanoni* [by Edward Bulwer-Lytton], which I don't like or understand at all it is so mystical, and then the captain came and took me all over the ship.

It is more than three times as long as dear old Mychunk [her home in Albemarle County, Virginia], and he showed me the huge anchors, and the signal cannon at the prow, with all the sails, the jib, fore topsail, top gallant sail, etc. He showed me the engines, the icehouse, the binnacle, the compass, the man steering the ship and everything and explained everything so kindly, without a bit of contempt for my ignorance as a landlubber. Then by means of a dizzy little ladder we gained the bridge where by the by no passengers are allowed to go, but he favors two of us, Mr. Lazarus

View on board ship in the 1880s showing ship's compass

and myself. Up there was the captain's own private cabin, a nice cozy little room, where we spent more than an hour while he elucidated to me the mysteries of the chronometer which keeps London time and enables them to tell in what longitude they are, the sextant, which shows the exact height of the sun, and the barometer. Then he showed me two large books, one by Maryatt showing the signal flags of all nations, and a code of signals made by different colored pennants which is the same all the world over. You can have no idea how varied and extensive they were, they amounted to over one million 8 thousand. They asked and answered every conceivable question from the most important to the most trivial, even one captain can signal to another by means of these flags, at a distance of ten miles, "Will you dine with me?" Isn't it wonderful?

The sailors all wear a short knife, like a butcher's in a belt round their waist, just behind, and their arms are covered with tattooing in all colors. I saw one this morning, who has two American flags and the eagles and all on one arm, and the other was equally covered though I could not make out the design. It is so strange to see them climbing up the rigging just like cats, up, up, until you can hardly distinguish them. They have been very busy all day, as we hope to make Kingston by tomorrow night, and they are getting ready to get the cargo out. A sailing vessel passed us early this morning but a long way off, still she looked like a large white bird on the blue water.

Mr. Weinshank has a magnificent Newfoundland dog on board named Carlo, he and I are great friends as he is as gentle as possible. How I shall miss dear old Taurus when I get home. I was too sick to realize about his going when he did, but now everything about home has an added interest. Everything there is more to me than anything else in the world. Even Jack would be a precious boon to me now, for he would have seen my darlings. I want Luly's picture so dreadfully I don't know what to do.

We shall see the mountains of Cuba *(Deo volente)* in another hour, and then we will have land in sight though distant until we reach Jamaica, which will be a great comfort, as both mind and body get so wearied of the immense expanse of water without anything to break its monotony. The sun sinks so suddenly behind the waves, but not into it as I have always read, it just gives you the impression of setting behind a huge blue hill.

They tell me that the loveliest flowers are made in Kingston of minute shells differently colored, and so perfect you think you can smell them. The people on board who have crossed before all unite in declaring Jamaica to be the most delightful country in the world, a land flowing with milk and honey. That is the country, but Kingston itself they unanimously say is horrid.

What do you think! The captain says both Mrs. and Miss Nash are colored people. That would rather shock Mr. Evans. He has known her for years and declares it is true and that I will meet dozens as fair as I am who yet have colored blood in their veins, and I may never find it out. They associate with the real whites, are very wealthy and only those who know the island well are cognizant of it.

The Italians have a curious musical instrument called a metallophone on which they play with two rubber balls on wire handles. It is about two feet and a half long, very narrow, with metal strips across the top like the keys of a piano, varying in tone from bass to treble. It is gilded and ornamented with bunches of flowers on the sides, rather too gaudy for my taste, but Mr. McAdam the captain's clerk takes great delight in playing on it. When he played "Nancy Lee" I could scarcely help crying it reminded me so of that day I left home coming to Keswick, when I felt as if each note would choke me. My one constant prayer day and night is that God would give me back my darlings again.

I would not be so homesick and despondent I think if I could only get well again, but sometimes I fear there is something radically wrong about me, and that I will never be well any more. I have suffered constant pain ever since I left home and of course that has depressed me. But if I could only always remember that,

"The present is all in God's keeping; the future his mercy shall clear."

And maybe God will let me get really well and strong and go back home to be a help to my darlings and not a burden to them. If they only knew how I regret every hasty word and selfish action now, because they were always so patient and gentle and unselfish with me. I cannot hear from home before the 23rd at the soonest, and I have been so anxious about dear Dab's ears ever since I left. If he were only going to be here with me in this warm climate to get cured.

I am so tired now I cannot write any more but you do not know my Journal what a comfort you have already become to me. You seem like a tie to the loved ones at Mychunk.

I watched the restless ocean
In its heaving to and fro
And it seemed a type of our busy life
With its burden of sin and woe
Our evil thoughts and fancies
Were like the raging waves
As midst their foam and fury
We seemed hastening to our graves.
I looked on the placid ocean
Bathed in the light of the sun
And it seemed a type of the endless rest
When our life on earth is done
Calmed were the gales of passion
Soothed were the waves of care
And the pure pale light of the evening sky
Seemed like an angel's prayer-
And instead of the storm and fury
Came a holy and peaceful calm
Till I felt as a little child at rest
In a loving Father's arm.
Oh! Lord when I reach Thy harbor
Bid the waves of my life be still
And while travelling over Life's ocean here
Teach me to know Thy will.

I know these lines are very poor, but they came into my head just now and I could not help writing them down.

The mountains of Cuba are in sight like a dim gray cloud, but something in their shape reminds me of the dear Blue Ridge. Mr. Lazarus lent me his opera glasses to look at them but to tell the truth I could not see anything with them, though of course I did not let him find it out. Now Kate Holladay has an exquisite pair, that were given her as a Xmas gift, mother of pearl and gold, and I could see beautifully with them.

Coaling a Steamship in Kingston, Jamaica,
The Illustrated London News, *1888.*

Friday Feb. 7th Kingston Jamaica

Tuesday evening as soon as I had finished writing, I was called out to see the lighthouse on Cape Mazy in Cuba. It looked like an enormous colossal statue, pure white and against a background of blue mountains. These rapidly became first gray and then green until we were quite close to them.

The formation of Cuba is very curious and evidently of volcanic origin. There is not a single curve but every terrace on the mountain slope is as regular as if cut by a knife. It is such a contrast to the mountains of Jamaica, which are, as the natives say, just like a pot boiling. When Queen Isabella asked Columbus to describe the island to her, he simply crumpled up a bit of paper in his hand and gave it to her saying "Behold it." And it is really just like it.

Soon after, we saw a great many flying fish, they are just like flocks of small white birds and fly farther than across our yard. Sometimes they fly on deck, but none came on board this voyage.

Wednesday morning was intensely hot, and spite of Uncle Will's warnings I found it impossible to retain my flannels, indeed everybody on board came out in summer garb. About noon we came in sight of the lighthouse on Cape Morant, and after that we steamed rapidly on up to Port Royal. First however we were boarded by a tiny pilot boat manned by a gibbering crew of blacks. It looked really frightful to see the little boat like a small white bird at the mercy of the waves, and with a crew that seemed quite demented. Off Port Royal we had to stop until the Dr., an old white bearded Scotchman, came on board to see if' there was any illness. His boat is compelled to hoist a yellow flag and he asked among other things if any of us had the Russian Plague.

A great contrast to his dugout boat with a negro crew, all shouting, was another boat from the guard ship which came to us. It was snowy white, with six stalwart English tars on board, dressed in white, with blue collars and anchors and white hats with blue ribbons, and legs and arms bare. It was just like an exquisite picture. The exquisite blue of the sea shading off into a delicate green as it neared the shore, and then again into white as the breakers rose and fell on the beach, the guard ship with every rope and sail in place, the many colored buoys all around and Port Royal in the background with its weather stained red brick houses, so curiously shaped some of them, and the tropical foliage waving in a gentle breeze. I think I should never tire of watching the cocoanut palms with the bunches of brown nuts all round the smooth grey stem, and the graceful, feathery, fern like leaves, never still for a moment.

After that we went up the harbor to Kingston, which is seven miles long and is considered one of the most beautiful in the world. I got very nervous then, as we were a day before our time and I was afraid no one would be there to meet me. The Countess and Marie now appeared most gorgeously arrayed. They had been to say the least of it quite slovenly all through the voyage, but now the Signora Patrizzio seemed determined to array herself according to her dignity, so she appeared in a claret colored cloth suit covered with ribbon bows and gold buttons, and invested herself with a pair of handsome diamond eardrops. It was quite the grub and the butterfly I assure you.

The captain and officers too assumed their uniform, and as the ship had been put into extra thorough rig and order, we made quite a gay sight with four flags flying. One was the union jack of England, another the star-spangled banner, then we had the U. S. mail flag and the company's pennant, so we were remarkably brave and gay.

I felt anything else however myself, I was so worn out by the heat and excitement and fear that I should not be met, but the captain put one of the mates to stay with me and keep any of the negroes or coolies from annoying me when the ship touched the pier as they swarmed all over her like bees in an instant.

Strange to say the tropical look of everything as I approached and could see up the streets of the city, was not at all strange or unusual to me, it was just the realization of what I had so often read, and seen pictures, that it was not as unreal as New York. There were lots of negro women in all colors of the rainbow, and the most astounding head handkerchiefs, all with panniers on their heads and every now and then a donkey.

The ship was soon full of men of all ages and colors, and what is so strange here, all on an equality. They are called brown ladies and gentlemen and move in the best circles. In the house opposite which is very handsome with marble statues in front of the entrance, and the court yard railed in with stone and wrought iron, there is an enormously wealthy girl (coal black) just going to marry a fair young Scotchman who only came out about twelve months ago. Money is certainly a great leveller, but my Virginia born eyes cannot get used to this equality of the races.

Well, just as I was on the verge of tears, Sophy and Mr. Evans appeared on the dock, in flowing robes of spotless white. By the way, the men mostly dress in white from the snowy white helmet which is universal to the spotless shoes, which would shame many a ladies white kid gloves. I believe they are made of cloth. They look very cool and nice.

Everybody drives here, indeed there are no sidewalks, and you have to go in the middle of the dusty street with the carriages, donkeys, negroes, and goats, of which there are a great number. The negro women have the funniest way of bending their knees by way of curtsying and they carry everything on their heads, which they do not tie up closely in their bandanna handkerchiefs as our servants but have them sticking out in horns and loops all round so they can scarcely get in at a door. I saw one coming up the street this morning in a white muslin through which her black skin was seen in high relief. Her sole burden was a cup and saucer which instead of carrying in her hand she bore on a board placed on her head while her hands were occupied in keeping her draperies, which were but scanty, out of the dust. Their feet and legs are invariably bare.

Whenever we ask the waiter for a glass of water she answers calmly, "Bey and bey." And it is by and by in reality, if you ever get it which is not often the case. Mr. Evans new saddle was stolen out of the stalls here the night I came and the police can get no clue to the thief, indeed they never can here. The lingo of the negroes and children here is perfectly heathenish and unintelligible. It is made up of every language and is entirely Greek to me.

King Street, Kingston, Jamaica, 1844

The custom house officers were very nice and gentlemanly. They simply asked if I had anything besides wearing apparel and never even unlocked my trunk. After waiting a long time for the coachman who had disappeared and was not forthcoming, we left the steamer and went to the carriage. A Mr. Pierce came with them who is a great friend of Mr. Evans. He is a married man of 47 with his right hand very badly twisted from having been badly set when broken. He was very polite and the next morning sent me a most exquisite bouquet of tea-roses and brilliant flowers. I have been wishing ever since I was magician enough to transport them into the dining room at home to delight the dear ones there.

I went straight to bed, I was so tired and saw no one but Sophy. I was terribly startled and nervous when I saw Mr. E on the deck but he behaved very well, he merely shook hands though I was really afraid he would have fallen, he turned so deadly pale. I have only seen him once since for about five minutes in the drawing room last night, as he is very considerate and has gone off with a Mr. Reid and will not be back before tomorrow night. And I find this Mr. Reid is a married man after all, and not a lover of Sophy's as we had thought. She is not at all well or strong, she nearly fainted this morning after dressing, and had to take wine and hartshorn. Her spirits are wretched too, I must try to cheer her if I can.

We are to stay here until Monday afternoon and then drive to Spanish town for the night on our way to the mountains. Sophy is so good to me she is almost, but not quite like one of my precious sisters in her looking after me. She is always bringing me beef tea, custard, wine, etc. and is very kind. She is much less reserved and more affectionate than I ever knew her.

We have a large room together on the ground floor, which is very cool comparatively speaking. 3 days ago I was dressed entirely in winter clothes and now I am panting in a thin white dress, and with flowers in my hair and bosom.

The houses here are about as high from the ground as the McIntire's, and then only one story. It gives them a very squat appearance. They are generally of red brick, and as far as I have seen are very much dilapidated, as to paint, locks etc. The drawing room floor however is more brilliantly polished than anything I ever saw. It is as bright as our dining table at home. There were some beautiful flowers there last night, tuberoses and geraniums, and orange blossoms. It was hard to realize it was February and probably the dear ones at home were shivering with cold. Oh! if they were only with me. I cannot enjoy anything without them.

The meals are as follows. At seven we have tea and a slice of bread and butter in our room. There we are expected to remain until ten when there is a meat breakfast without either tea or coffee, only water, and then nothing more until dinner at seven when you are expected to dress and go in with gentlemen's arms etc. I have not seen a bit of fruit of any kind since I left the ship except on the trees. Indeed I have been in my bedroom most of the time and have never left the house. Sophy is lying down and keeps begging me to stop writing and do the same, and as I am still very weak I think I had better take her advice.

Letter home to Margaret, Lucy, and Dabney Trice from Martha Jefferson Trice, Hanover St., Kingston, Jamaica, February 8, 1879

My precious darlings,

What would not I give for a sight of your dear dear faces, instead of writing! but I know you want to know all about my journeyings so however unsatisfactory, I must try to tell you of them on paper.

In the first place here I am safely landed and watched over by Sophy with dragon-like care. Cousin Waller, Willie, Kate, and Katie went with me to the ship and after they left me my heart very nearly failed me entirely. I staid below in a horrid little hole of a cabin until evening when I went on deck, but it was bitterly cold so I soon retreated to the little deck cabin , a room about the size of the little room, which was our only place to sit except the dining salon as the *Etna* was only built for a merchant vessel and the accommodations were both limited and very uncomfortable.

There were two other ladies!! on board besides myself, an Italian Countess and a French woman who did not understand one word or English. The Italian woman, Signora Patrizzio, did talk a very little broken English, but even if they had been fluent, I could not have associated with them as they were the lowest kind of actresses and, with a Frenchman who accompanied them formed part of a troupe that are acting here. They were dreadful people, so I rarely spoke to them beyond a *bonjour* in the morning. Then there was a horrid Anglo-American hybrid from Nassau and these with two Finns and a German Jew from New York, Mr. Weinshank, and a London Jew, Mr. Lazarus, comprised our company.

There was only one, Mr. Lazarus, who had any pretensions to gentility and he was really very nice and exceedingly kind to me. He is enormously wealthy, about 50, and very like Cousin Will. He is very tall and stalwart but was born with only four fingers on his left hand and on his right the arm just dwindles to one finger. He seems to have no trouble, however, and does everything for himself.

Then there was a very handsome young man, the captain's clerk, Mr. McAdam, just my age but he looks quite a boy. He and Mr. Lazarus were my sole associates, with the exception of my kind, good captain. He was a nice gray bearded man named Ferguson and he was really just like a father to me. He rarely ever left my side from the time I hobbled up the companion ladder, just after day in the morning, until he helped me down at eleven at night, for I never went below all day, I was not able. He did not like to leave me alone with the foreigners so he sat just by me as I lay flat on the couch and read to me and told me long histories of his life and wrecks and anything he thought would amuse me and even went and brought me beef tea and chicken broth himself. I never knew greater kindness.

I think for a day or two he was rather afraid I might vanish from his gaze for I was very ill for two days. I could scarcely lift my hand. Not from seasickness for I was only seasick about 38 hours. Indeed, they thought me a remarkably good sailor, but the motion of the cars on to Washington caused another abscess to form and from Wednesday until Monday I suffered horribly. The motion of the ship seemed to increase the pain very much.

We had a beautiful passage, a day shorter than any had ever been known before, which I maintained was entirely owing to Uncle Phil's prayers in my behalf. It rained however on Saturday and Sunday and the sea was very rough, indeed. Though we had a strong wind and came very fast, that very fact caused the ship to roll and pitch a great deal. Three days we were first on our heads and then on our feet as first ceiling and then floor were uppermost, but it did not make me seasick though nearly every other passenger was. The captain said I did not have enough stamina to be seasick. Well by Sunday evening there was so much sea we got quite drenched, even in the deck cabin and I thought I should be blown off the deck that night going down stairs. However, by Mr. Lazarus' and the captain's aid, that catastrophe was averted and Monday morning showed us a beautiful day with a calm sea and the air very warm. After that it was very pleasant.

We had the awning spread on deck and everybody was so kind to me from the captain to the cabin boy. They were at my beck and call, or, as the little Frenchman said, "Mees, we is all your sarvantes."

Please, my darlings, don't think me very egotistical and vain but I was the only <u>lady</u> on board and travelling alone, so they all petted me. Monday night I went down to dinner and received quite an ovation. Everybody wanted to drink wine with me and the captain asked me to order drinks next day, which honor I declined with haste and trepidation. Mr. Lazarus had brought some very fine oranges with him and with these he plied me from morning till night, how I wished for you all, for somehow in the suffering I have unaccountably lost my boasted appetite, but it will soon come back now I am safely on land.

Tuesday the captain took me all over the ship and showed me the sextant, chronometer, and all the ins and outs of navigation and even invited me into his room, where I spent a very pleasant hour looking over all the flags and pennants of all the ships of different nations with him to explain their meaning. He is devoted to reading and has travelled everywhere and fairly worships Dickens, all of whose works he has by heart, so being thrown entirely on each other for society, we became the greatest chums imaginable. I told him I was certainly going back with him, spite of the uncomfortable ship, which you know is not his fault. The Atlas, being the only line, has the monopoly and does not try to make the passengers comfortable but they are going to put on two new ships in the summer.

Tuesday we saw the island of Cuba and the lighthouse on Cape Mazy which looked like a huge white statue against the blue mountains. I enjoyed seeing land again as you may imagine after so much water, and being accommodated with Mr. Lazarus' deck chair and opera glass, passed a very pleasant evening, though rather too warm. Then, too, the captain fished me up some gulfweed which I am saving for you and I saw some flying fish which are like tiny white birds and fly as far as across our yard.

Wednesday morning, spite of dear Uncle Will's cautions, I could no longer retain my flannels as it was oppressively hot and all the gentlemen appeared in white linen. We sighted Jamaica at 9 o'clock, or two bells in nautical phraseology and after that everything was just lovely. The sea was black the first day and then very dark blue indeed, but this day it became so very beautiful, shifting its colors like a kaleidoscope, the most delicate blue then pale green with purple shadows and the snowy breakers on the beach in the distance. How I longed for you all, but really, there has not been an hour since I left home that I have not done that, except when it was rough and I thought you would be frightened, I only wanted Dabney then, he would have enjoyed it.

After a while we saw the lighthouse on Cape Morant and then we drew nearer the island and passed swiftly up the coast by fields of sugarcane, such a delicate tender green with white houses nestling in the trees. It looked like our own dear mountains beneath a summer sun.

When we reached Port Royal, the Dr. came off to us with a yellow flag which is the regulation but which struck terror to my heart and asked if there had been any contagious illness on board. There too came the Lieutenant from the guard ship all ornate and gay with his gold hilted sword and handsome uniform in a boat manned with real English Tars, just exactly like we have so often seen pictures of and read of. There we saw the first cocoanut trees, so feathery and fernlike with clusters of nuts around the trunk.

I got very nervous and downhearted with all the noise and excitement and I was so afraid nobody might meet me. Then we went up Kingston harbor which is considered the most beautiful one almost in the world, and strange to say, as yet what I have seen of the Tropics, seems so very natural instead of strange. It is so like what we have read of and seen pictures of, the darkeys and palms etc., it did not seem nearly as unreal as New York.

We were all in gala attire by this time with flags flying and the captain in uniform and the foreigners, who had been slovens up to this time, appearing perfect butterflies. The harbor was filled with shipping and I saw several very fine boats, but I was too tired and anxious then to enjoy them. But all my fears were soon set at rest by the appearance of Mr. Evans and Sophy in glowing robes of spotless white. They were delighted to see me as they had been waiting several days for me and were going to wait till the next steamer if I had not come.

Mr. E. did not attempt to do what I feared, but I was really afraid he would faint when he shook hands with me, he turned so deadly pale. Sophy looks well but she is not at all strong, she eats literally nothing and nearly fainted yesterday morning after dressing. She is more affectionate than I ever saw her and not one bit screwed, just the reverse. She is always bringing me beef tea, etc. and is just as lovely and kind as anybody could be to me but, my dear sisters! we share the same room and stay in it all the time as Mr. E. has very considerately gone into the country and I have only seen him once. He comes back tonight and we leave here Monday for Malvern.

I have seen literally nothing since I reached here, I have not left the house so, though already much better, I am still very weak and have spent most of my time on the bed. It is very warm. I am panting in a **lamé** dress. Sophy has given me two pretty white checked muslin princess dresses. I have only seen one, the dressmaker came just now to try it on. She had them cut before I came by her patterns and had to make some alterations. The dressmaker was a tall mulatto or brown lady as they are invariably called here, in a handsome black silk trimmed with lace and who fitted me with a pair of white kids on, and came in her carriage. They are received in the best society here but are quite a lower class in the mountains.

The cooking here is horrid and they greatly affect curries. I have not yet seen a single fruit, but a Mr. Pierce sent me a most beautiful bouquet of tea roses, tuberoses, geraniums, etc. in which I have revelled. How I wish I could send it to you. He is a married man I met the first evening.

Mr. Reid is coming tonight to see us but to my amazement he too is married and has children. We have tea at seven in our rooms, at ten a meat breakfast, and at seven a dinner when you are expected to dress and take gentlemen's arms, etc. I shall be so glad when we are safely at Malvern.

I must send this now as I will not be able to write after I get there as the steamer will have left. Give my dearest, dearest love to everybody, and don't forget the servants, tell Granny to keep well and strong until I get back. I cannot understand one word the servants here say, it is like Greek.

Instead of feeling uneasy at sea, even when it was rough, I never felt so completely safe in a Heavenly Father's care in my life. The very fact of being such an atom in the infinite took all the self conceit and dread out of me for I felt there was then no reliance on human aid.

My darlings, don't overwork yourselves, you must take care of yourselves for my sake, you cannot think how I yearn for you all. I shall enclose a note to the Dr. Sampsons in this same postage. With dear love to the Davises, Minors, Sampsons, and everybody indeed.

Your loving sister
May God guard my precious ones for me.

Monday Feb. l0th, Kingston

My spare time for the last two days has been taken up in writing letters to the dear home people, and seeing a good deal of Sophy whose spirits are very much depressed, so that I spend a good deal of time trying to cheer her up.

Yesterday I was much amused when Nana, the woman who brought me in some dinner, went to take out the plate. There was a tray just beside her, but instead she preferred setting the plate on top of her brilliant bandanna and marching off. I am afraid I should not have felt as much amused if she had brought it in that way.

There are some people boarding here for a few days, who have come in from the country. They are a Mr. and Mrs. Davidson. He is a coffee planter and is enormously wealthy, and one of the first men in the island. He is nothing else but a colored man, just as brown as can be imagined and his wife is colored too. And still their niece, who is with them, is as delicately fair as possible. One difference in the colored people here and in America, is that there, they are either black, gingerbread, or yellow, and here they are really brown, without a tinge of yellow, but with rather a red tinge under the skin.

Yesterday evening we walked just down to the end of this street to call on a Mr. and Mrs. Pierce, who the Evans know, and who have left cards for me and sent those lovely flowers the other day. He is headmaster of the Mico School here, and is a nice clever man, and she has particularly winning manners. It was my first experience of Kingston, and I felt very funny in my best dress and slippers to be walking down the middle of a street 3 inches deep in dust, and every few steps having to leap over an evil smelling sewer, but it was such a very short distance it would have been silly to have had the carriage.

Mrs. Pierce showed me some very artistically grouped ferns, gold and silver, which her mother had pressed and framed. I must try to get some to do for the girls. After we had had coffee which it is always considered etiquette to offer here at night as they never have supper, Mr. Pierce took us out into his garden and showed us so many curious trees which have hitherto been only names to me. I saw the banana which grows something like a reed but with the leaves only at the top, each leaf about 4 or 5 feet long and all in one perfectly smooth and green. That is one thing I observe here, the leaves being so smooth and polished, with none of the down of our trees, but much more like evergreens. Then I saw the pimento or allspice, the breadfruit with its large hand-shaped leaves, an orange tree with the young fruit, sugar cane, and finally some cocoa palms. These he planted himself 7 years ago and they had been bearing for 2 years.

A curious old man was there, half a lunatic, a Mr. Ford, and Mr. Pierce asked him to climb the tree and get us some young cocoanuts. Instantly to my horror he sprung up the smooth pyramidal shaped trunk and as you know the huge fern like leaves spring from the very top of the trunk, I expected him down on our heads every moment. But he very calmly caught one of the leaves themselves, and though it creaked and bent, still it did not give way, and he very coolly returned handing us each an oval green fruit about 4 inches long. Of course it was too young to be eatable, indeed I am beginning to agree with the "Tropical Fallacy" about Jamaica fruit, for "niver a bit" have I seen since I got here, though all the passengers raved about this being a perfect Canaan, and talked incessantly of custard apples, shaddocks, granadillas and a dozen other names I cannot remember. Perhaps I shall see them before I leave.

We are to go on to Spanish Town tonight, and there are two remarkably fine cottonwood trees on the way there, the finest in the island. Sophy showed me some such curious bark she got in one of the shops here. It is called lace bark, and is just like cream colored net of different degrees of fineness. By steeping it in soda and water it becomes purely white, and fichus are made of it. She saw a bonnet made for the Paris Exhibition made

Coconut Palm, 1897

of the dagger plant, a kind of cactus with immensely long leaves, one side green and the other white. These they split and weave into hats. This was a bridal bonnet trimmed with veils of this lace bark and dagger plant roses, and she describes it as lovely.

Mr. Evans brought us some pieces of sugar cane and a bottle of the juice. It was simply horrid. He said it had been delicious two hours before, and was sour then, but I recognized the same disagreeable after-taste that sorghum has. He brought some bundles of sugar too, directly from the estate where it was manufactured. One parcel was just about the color of maple sugar, and a little like it in taste, and the other which Sophy pronounced very fine, was indeed beautifully granulated, and very sweet but very much darker than our usual brown coffee sugar. Strange to say white sugar here is hard to get and very high, as though the sailors' old story of Jamaica's having mountains of sugar, and rivers of rum is very nearly true, yet for want of proper refineries, all the best sugar is carried to England, refined there, and then brought back here, and sold to the natives at two prices. Jamaica is asleep, but the new governor Sir Anthony Musgrave is a very judicious man and is setting slowly but surely to work to remedy the abuses.

Sophy has given me two white dresses trimmed with embroidery, it is too warm here for anything else. God has given me such kind friends. When this journey was first contemplated we seemed scarcely able to provide the necessaries for it, and now everything has been supplied by my darlings and my kind good friends, until I have everything in the dress line I need.

The dressmaker who came to try on my dress was a mulatto woman, but here a brown lady, dressed in a handsome black silk, with white kids, which she retained while fitting my dress, and she came in her carriage with a little maid to bring in her parcels. I felt quite abashed in the presence of so grand a demoiselle. She has visited Europe and is called Miss Piexotto. Even the servants are called Miss or Mrs. here by their mistresses.

Mrs. Lillie, the lodging house keeper, a very respectable woman with seven children, whose husband was a judge, and died leaving her so poor she had to take boarders, said yesterday, "Miss Evans, how did you like the lady who used to cook for your mamma? Mrs. Brisbane I mean." Sophy did not know who she meant for some time.

Mr. Pierce sent me some flowers again this morning that came from a pen out in the country, oleanders, roses and others that are beautiful but I do not know their names. All the plantations here are called pens. Mr. Evans is thinking of buying one of them, a large sugar estate called Rozelle, but all his friends here advise him not to do it, as it is considered very unhealthy being near a lagoon. I hope if he does buy it, it will be after I have left, for as to staying here as he hopes, it is entirely out of the question. I am afraid he is going to be a large drop of bitter in my cup while I am here, for though he is very kind and good, I begin almost to hate him when he gets sentimental and he can make me uncomfortable for hours, when I am reading, by just sitting off and gazing at me all the time. Of course reading under such circumstances is impossible, and I just want to put down my book and make faces at him. I know such feelings are very wrong but he really does worry me so much. I have told him so often I never could be his wife that the sooner he believes it the better for him and for me too, as he renders my life a burden to me.

I sent off my first letters to my darlings today. I wish I was going with them, but with everybody so kind to me, I must try to put away such feelings of homesickness or at least not let them see them. Oh! no one knows how I pine for my sisters and dear little Dab. I must pack my trunk now for the steamer that is to take it to Black River up in the mountains, so I must tell you goodbye for the present my dear Journal, this travelling about upsets all regular hours for writing.

Cutting sugar cane in Jamaica

Spanish Town, Feb 11th 1879

We left Kingston yesterday evening about five o'clock, we were to have left at three, but Mr. Evans was delayed, and we could not get off. The road for about a mile out of Kingston was so dusty we could scarcely breathe and the cactus hedges on either side were perfectly grey with the dust. I could not help being reminded again of the "Tropical Fallacy" but after about a mile the road grew firm and hard and as smooth as a bowling green, and driving became very pleasant. My kind friends had put a board from the front to the back seat of the carriage so that I could lie down, and as the carriage is an open one I could see out very well.

My view was entirely confined to the road itself, as the cactus hedges were twelve or eighteen feet high and formed a complete boundary. Yet still I saw a good many queer things in the road. An old man with a huge trunk on his head, as if it were nothing, an aged woman in only a chemise and very short white skirt with a gay bandanna on her head, and a large basket filled with yams, then a donkey cart, piled high with guinea grass and three or four young negro men with straw sundown hats and the inevitable bright handkerchief tied around it, formed a very gay picture. Even the men invariably wear these handkerchiefs on their heads, and the old, old women wear them, and hats on top. Never a sunbonnet by any chance, and such scanty garments. Yet I must say they are generally scrupulously clean. We would meet laborers returning home, in nothing but a tattered shirt and drawers, but as white as possible. I do not know if the fact of its being Monday had anything to do with it.

We saw the cottonwood trees, though not very well, as there is no twilight in Jamaica, and before we reached them the lamps had to be lighted to the carriage, yet we threw the light on them as well as we could. They were really enormous in girth, though not very tall, but their shape is most remarkable. The trunk of the tree is divided in cells or caves, so large a man might sit comfortably in them and then such knotted misshapen branches. They are the largest in the island and are called first and second specimen. We travelled very fast as Rhoda and Jessie, Mr. Evans' two mules, are really very fine handsome animals, rather too spirited for a coward like myself.

We saw such flocks of goats on our way, they milk them here constantly. One thing that constantly depresses one in Jamaica is the look of ruin and desolation spread over everything. Next a comfortable house will be a miserable tumbledown thatched hut, of one room with a door of wattles, and surrounded with a rank growth of mangroves. The fences are

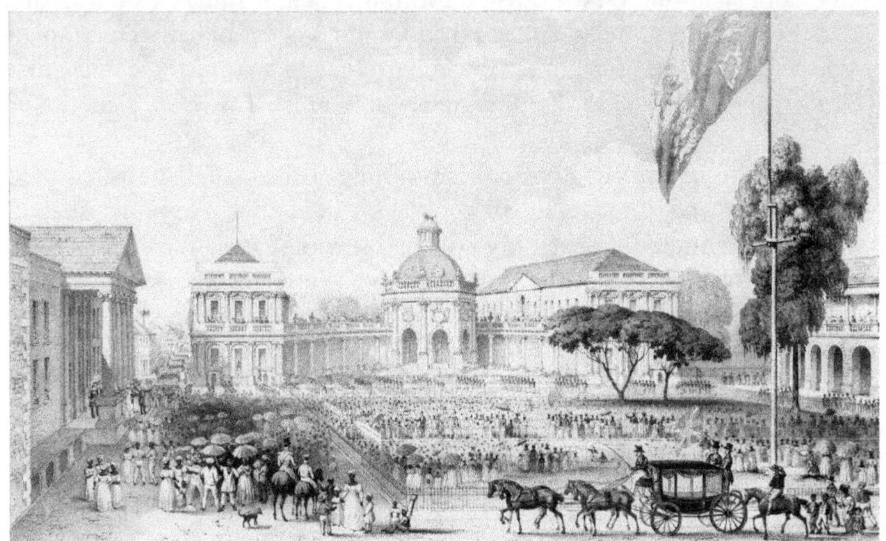

Spanish Town, Jamaica on August 1, 1838 - the day slavery was abolished

made of rotten boards all falling down and decaying. The better houses have always a high brick or stone wall like a jail with a huge entrance gate for carriages with a lamp over the entrance and a small gate on either side. I am reminded so often of the pictures of Moorish architecture.

We reached here at nine last night and are staying at a Miss Lane's Lodgings. She has a very handsome place, beautifully clean and large, and with the handsomest mahogany doors I ever saw. In the drawing room there is an arch so beautifully carved and black with age. And then the furniture in our bedroom is of such a beautiful polish. It is all very old and was brought from Spain. Indeed the Spanishtonians are quite grandees, and look down on the Kingstonians. This house is very well kept, and the cooking is a great improvement on Kingston. Still I find it hard to get used to seeing such quantities of red pepper, capsicums, onions and limes all mixed up with the meats.

I saw some such gorgeous flowers this morning, they are in reality long narrow leaves, the most beautiful shade of red with a soft down all over them. They are however terribly infested with ants, indeed yesterday evening, I held a bouquet in my lap all the way here and I became completely covered with ants. The mosquitoes too are very bad, I awoke this morning with my face speckled over with red spots. But one comfort is the entire absence of flies.

The houses are kept very dark, indeed the most wretched negro huts have shutters. The windows as a rule do not run up but open in the middle like a door, with the blinds outside forming a small, square low window. I like this plan very much, and shall adopt it if I ever am called on to plan a house. Miss Lane is a mulatto woman rather like Aunt Rose and quite yellow, yet this is the best lodging house in Spanish Town.

I saw the *lignum vitae* tree this morning. It has small polished pale green leaves and is covered all over with pale lilac blossoms shaped rather like a buttercup. Yesterday now and then in the cactus hedges were great trees of pink and white oleanders, but we could not perceive their fragrance, as the road from Kingston here is through the marshes, and the mangroves give a rank unhealthy odor, which is productive of fever and malaria.

Mr. Evans gave me yesterday a great package of blue paper and envelopes, a crown piece with a ring to hang it around the neck, and a very handsome book, *Seawards Narrative*. I did not want to take them but he vowed he would throw them in the street if I did not. Sophy too only this morning gave me a copy of *Ancient and Modern Hymns*, which I have wanted for a long time. She is just like a sister to me. She has improved greatly I think since I knew her in Virginia. She has had a great deal of sorrow, and it has made her so gentle and unselfish. I wish my troubles could have a like effect.

There is a cactus just outside the door, with leaves like our prickly pear, though much larger, but instead of running on the ground and having yellow blossoms, it is quite a tree with rose colored flowers and small green figs. There is an orange tree also but the fruit is all green and small and there are no flowers on it. I find it so hard to describe the numerous trees I see as I have never seen anything like them and do not know what to compare them with.

I never saw such numbers of lizards as at this house, they are every color and circulate freely through the windows, and rooms. Aloes are very much used for hedges, imagine miles of roads bordered with century plants. Oh! I have eaten cassava cakes. There came in this morning at breakfast three small thin cakes folded like an envelope. They were crisp and hard and had a pleasant taste. They are sold in the streets though are not plentiful.

Today the ship sails from America, and in ten days more I hope to hear from home. God grant I may not have any bad news, but it has been nearly three weeks since I left them and I cannot help feeling very anxious and uneasy until I hear. We left Spanish Town Tuesday evening, and I was very much amused by Miss Lane just before we left. As we were standing in the door waiting for the carriage to be packed, a handsome buggy drove up and out stepped a nice looking young man who greeted Miss Lane most cordially and carried on a whispered conversation for a few moments. As soon as he had driven away, she said, "Dat ees Airnest Fillippo me godson." He was as we knew, white, and the son of an Italian physician in Kingston.

The young man had just returned from England, and she remarked, "Airnest ees grown queet black, he used to be feer clair looking." "Had you mooch reen een the heells, Miss Evans? Two weeks ago we had so mooch reen, that my mamma died and we had to deeg two graves before we could get a dry one for her." She said this with the utmost calmness, and was dressed in a pink and brown lawn skirt, with a red and white handkerchief round her neck, and was in excellent spirits.

We then drove on towards Old Harbor, seeing on the road a boy coming from school dragging a serpent 10 feet long and as thick as my arm which he had just killed.

The negro women always tie a string just above their hips which raises their dresses in a bunch there and shortens it to the knees, and as both men and women even the very old never wear shoes, the display of their pedal extremities is excessive. It makes such an ungraceful hump all round them. They either wear very bloomer like costumes, or very long trains sweeping in the dirt and filth of the road. I saw some Malay coolies too, handsome olive colored men with much better countenances than the Jamaican negroes, who are really the most sullen, discontented looking set of people I ever saw, out of the hundreds we have met on the road I have not seen one smiling or pleasant looking. I think it is because they are envious of others of their own color who are their mistresses and are received in society, for Sophy has remarked the same thing too.

The Malays all have turbans just like the one we read of in the Arabian nights which the roc carried away for her nest, and then they either wear a short jacket of red and yellow, and a tunic, or else only a red or blue shirt, "Only that and nothing more." I think constantly how horrified Mildred would be if she could see many of these people. I saw the other day a very antiquated specimen of humanity, in the shape of a dilapidated old negro, just emerging from a tiny hut made of wattles and thatched with cocoanut leaves, clothed only in a breech cloth, and a "sad sweet smile." Some of the children have the smile without the cloth I am told but I have not seen any yet.

Old Harbor is simply the very most dreadful place I ever was in. It is about as large as Milton [a village near Charlottesville, Va.] and is a collection of filthy decaying huts, and a conglomeration of the most fearful smells imaginable. We slept a little out of the town at the best house the place affords, the worst house in Palmyra [a small town near Charlottesville, Va.] would have been a palace in comparison, but we had fresh air which was something. It is kept by a Mrs. Harrison, a fat dirty black woman whose two boldfaced, brazen looking mulatto daughters strutted about the house like peacocks, and gave up for our benefit their bed room, a stuffy crowded little room with holes as large as my head in the floor, one of which, the largest, was modestly covered with a goatskin as the family slept beneath us, and I firmly believe about a dozen goats as well, which we had seen grazing in the yard. I am convinced they were very near us from the peculiar goaty smell of everything about our room. I had to saturate my nightgown with cologne before I could sleep.

The food was dirty and badly cooked so we were delighted to make an early start the next morning. In both Spanish Town and Old Harbor were pictures stuck up and flaming advertisements of my quondam travelling companion Madame Patrizzio, who was to come in a few days. I cannot say I felt any sorrow at leaving her behind.

We now passed through huge fields of sugar cane, so thickly planted it seemed impossible to squeeze through it, it is worked by hand, but labor is quite cheap here nominally, as men work for an English shilling a day, but they do not begin work until seven and leave off at four, so that really it is expensive in the end.

We saw some laborers on the road carrying stones, and whereas our laborers would have used a wheelbarrow, these men had a half bushel basket of them on their heads. They all have a cutting knife somewhat shaped like the Malayan cruse, as they could never penetrate the forests without it; they are so matted together with cacti, lianas and creepers of a thousand sorts. Sometimes a tree will be covered with ten or twelve different kinds of leaves or flowers, and you do not know which are the original sort, or perhaps the tree itself, though a living mass of verdure, is dead, killed by its numerous parasites. I saw one yesterday with yellow, white, and scarlet trumpets on it and at least half a dozen different cacti, some hanging down in ropes and clusters 80 feet long without any apparent sustenance.

After we got about 14 miles from Old Harbor, the scenery became truly tropical. The road wound along the side of a steep mountain with beetling cliffs of a limestone formation and covered with a complete lacework of drooping delicate ferns, and going far back in places into mimic grottoes and caves that were filled with flowers, ferns, bright green lizards etc. and on the other hand was a precipice of several hundred feet, in some places protected by a parapet, in others open, and our wheels at times approached dangerously near the edge. Down far, far below was a valley, but so filled with huge trees and vines that it was one bewildering mass of foliage with now and then a break showing plantations of bananas and a river winding in a tortuous manner as a "wounded snake draws its slow length along."

Then suddenly the scene would change, the road would be lined with cocoanut trees, fan palms, mangoes, which have leaves like the ivy and flowers like the sumack, and are very handsome trees. Then would be a huge cotton wood tree completely draped with cacti, with scarlet blossoms, and with its gaunt crooked limbs far above its fellows, for as a rule the tropical trees, though very tall, are very small in girth, and a large one looks unusual. Then we would pass groups of wattled huts, half buried in cocoanuts, bananas, and orange trees with gaily dressed negro women, and half naked children staring at us, and half-starved curs rushing out.

One very sad thing here is the terrible emaciation of the horses, mules, donkeys, dogs and pigs. They are evidently so ill treated, having raw sores, and so very very thin, I never saw anything like it. They have only two kinds of vehicles here, carriages or buggies, and horsecarts which have one pitiful little donkey or mule in the shafts and one tied by ropes on either side, and all three so dreadfully weak and abused they can scarcely draw the cart along. Women ride the donkeys very often seated on the panniers, and it would look very pretty and picturesque if one could get over their pity for the poor animals.

They carry the wearing of bright handkerchiefs here to such an extent that even children of one and two wear them, and some not more than six months old, who were seated astride on their mothers' hips, as they trudged back from market, had them on. We passed through orchards of orange trees laden with fruit, and I saw one tree on the mountain side as large as our catalpa, covered with the golden globes, but as a rule they are about one third larger than the cherry tree in the back yard at home. They grow wild too, all over the mountains and the cocoanut trees were laden with ripe fruit, but we swept relentlessly by them all, until I felt like the Ancient Mariner.

One scene we saw was particularly pretty. It was down a deep ravine on the mountain side. There was a river in which stood a horseman talking to three women in bright pink and white dresses who were standing in the river busily washing with stones.

We often passed by wayside stores which consisted merely of a long narrow shed closed on three sides, with the fourth open to the road, and displaying numerous bottles of spirits, ale etc. ranged on the shelves interspersed with sardine boxes and a few tins and gay prints, or sometimes the wares were merely ranged on the mud floor with the owner sitting cross-legged beside them. Yet these stores make an unheard of amount of money. I saw one, a mere shed something like a cow shelter, where the proprietor made $150.00 every month.

We often passed blacksmith, shoemakers and carpenter shops, sometimes only 4 poles stuck in the ground with a roof of palm thatch; but whoever we passed, and whatever they were doing, they always stopped to gaze at us until we passed and then resumed their work with the utmost insouciance. They are the laziest people I ever saw.

We stopped for some coffee at Porus, and also to meet the horses that had been sent down to us from Mandeville, for the mules were quite broken down by this time. Porus is a collection of squalid negro huts, not nearly as good as Aunt Rose' s cabin, but in the best of these, about as good as our old schoolhouse, we stopped to rest a little, and escape a drenching shower. We were shown into a tiny bed room, but the bed was too uninviting to tempt us, so we only waited until the rain commenced to slacken a little, and then set off in grand style. We had three horses with a postillion on the front one and then Russell, the Evans' groom, rode just in front of him with the two mules. The horses were quite fresh so we fairly tore up and down hill for fifteen miles to Mandeville, but we went so very fast and the roads were so very good it did not seem more than 5 miles.

I have never in my wildest dreams imagined such roads. We have come already sixty miles and have climbed this mountain two thousand five hundred feet above the sea level and we have never seen in the road a rock or a gully. Even the little branches no larger than our barn branch will have an immensely high iron bridge much longer than the one going into Charlottesville. I did not at all understand it at first but it is because in the rainy season these little streams become perfect torrents and spread far out on every side, and as this is a royal mail road, allowances have to be made for every kind of weather.

We reached here in a pouring rain and are staying in a delightfully clean and well kept house belonging to a Miss Roy, an old maiden lady (colored of course). I have not met more than three whites since we left Kingston and at least 500 colored people, many in handsome carriages. We met two brides dressed in white lace and muslin with buff kid gloves and shoes and white veils and a great profusion of pink flowers and ribbons all over them. They were bareheaded and had Mexican blankets spread over the back of the buggies, red yellow and green in squares.

This morning a white lady strikingly like Mrs. Brisco came to call on Miss Roy, and they seemed very intimate. Everything is so well served here and the linen is so white and the silver so bright and shining it is a pleasure to sit down to table. My darlings at home could hardly realize a *"dame de coulour"* possessing two sets of silver tea services and having massive silver candlesticks. She has too a very pretty garden with a number of' rare plants in it.

Yesterday coming here we saw such lovely convolvuli climbing all over the trees of different hues, and a lovely scarlet bell shaped flower called the shoeblack, as it polishes shoes beautifully. The coffee plant is extremely pretty with small dark green leaves and sprays of star like white flowers growing all down the twigs like a wreath and very fragrant. I saw some too with the berry, like an oval red cherry, in which are the seeds. The coffee is almost always good in Jamaica.

We leave here early tomorrow morning, and will not stop again except to put in fresh horses until we reach Ivor cottage which we hope to do tomorrow evening, but it has been raining so hard all day I am afraid the roads will be heavy.

When we were tearing along so rapidly yesterday evening, I felt like St. Nicholas and his reindeer:

> *"To the top of the house to the top of the wall*
> *Now dash away, dash away, dash away all."*

The air is deliciously cool and fresh up here, of course we wear thin dresses, but last night for the first time we put a thin blanket over our feet and did not find it uncomfortable. I find the carriage very comfortable as my couch is arranged with such care and I do not wear any corset, and lie down a good deal, but I confess I was rather glad of today's rest, on Sophy's account as well as my own. She is so patient and gentle with her brother, her manners are just lovely to him. He is exceedingly irritable and quite frightens me by flying into a passion at every little trifle and she soothes him so sweetly it is quite a lesson to me. She is so altered, and tries so hard to do her duty.

The days here are quite unsatisfactory in regard to their length. In summer in Va., the sun rises between 4 and 5, and here where it is warmer it does not rise until nearly seven, and the instant the sun sets at about six it is entirely dark, without any twilight.

This house is just on the side of the road, you step from the carriage to the steps, and as we breakfast in the front room, and there are no halls here, we are exposed to anybody's gaze who chooses to look at us. At least half a dozen carriages passed while we were at table this morning and innumerable foot passengers. But privacy is unknown in Jamaica. Sometimes half the wall is made of lattice work, and I have seen numbers of houses, large ones too, composed of the roof and walls entirely made of Venetian blinds. Sophy had to sleep for three weeks when she first landed in a room of this fashion. A large room had been divided into two by a thin partition of planks only seven feet high, merely a screen in fact. She occupied one half, and two young American men the other. Pleasant wasn't it? But all the partitions here are as "thin as pasteboard" and every sound can be heard from one room to the other. Only the other night at Old Harbor, it was so disagreeable we could not sleep and Sophy undertook to tell me some marvelous stories of travelling on the continent, some of her own experience and some of her Mother's, and I was in a perfect agony, lest Mr. Evans should hear her as he was in the next room, and that, here, is almost equivalent to being in the same.

A scene in Jamaica, 1891

Ivor Cottage Feb 18th 1879. Jamaica

Just opposite to our lodging house in Mandeville there was a large government hospital in whose grounds a number of convicts were at work and I was quite touched by hearing them singing Moody and Sankey's hymns when they stopped for their dinner. It reminded me of home to hear "Hold the Fort", and "Bright Jewels". Miss Russell's hymnbooks would have been acceptable, I do not doubt. The convicts passed just before our door dragging horse carts, and they seemed mostly young men, with good countenances.

We left on Friday morning, and got here at 5 o'clock the same evening. The road was so very steep the last day that we became terribly fatigued even though part of the time we had four mules, but they were so small, weak and ill-used they literally could not pull us up the mountain and Sophy and I walked almost a mile in consequence.

We saw a magnificent view from the top of a mountain called Spurtree Hill, which we crossed. We descended from Mandeville, two thousand, five hundred feet into a valley where it was intensely hot, such a change from the cool pure air of the mountain. There we were met by the emaciated mules at a pen called Pepper from its great heat. It is an immense grazing farm, and we saw a number of really fine cattle and horses. The cows were very large and have enormous branching horns, which the people often have polished and put in their houses as we do stags' horns. We met a drove of cattle, about one hundred, and they were haltered two and two by ropes round the neck, and driven by half a dozen whooping, screaming, shouting negroes. It seems impossible for the Jamaica negroes to do anything quietly. They are always screaming "Yah, yah" when driving. The women always wear hats on top of their wonderful head handkerchiefs, even down to the babies, they would not wear a sunbonnet on any account.

Everything is immensely high here, for instance, Glycerine is 25 cents per ounce, and they always charge extra for the bottle. To stamp a .letter to America is 12 cents, while, strange to say from America here is only 5 cents.

Dear Mrs. Evans was out some distance from the house to meet me, as she had descried us descending the mountain. These mountains, the Santa Cruz, are two thousand three hundred feet above the sea, and this cottage is 3 hundred feet from the summit. I observed tears in the dear old lady's eyes when she embraced me, and she told me afterwards, it was because of my great likeness to my precious Mother. Daisy welcomed me just as she did Sophy, kissed and embraced me, so that from my kind reception I felt at home immediately.

I have, in my opinion, the pleasantest room in the house. It is very large and cool with 3 large windows, from two of which is the most exquisitely beautiful view imaginable. There is the green plain two thousand feet below us, covered with forests, and broken every now and then by a cluster of white cottages, among which winds the road to Black River, fifteen miles distant, like a crumpled yellow ribbon. Embosomed among the trees are two large ponds, one Saltpond, Where great quantities of salt are made annually, and the other Alligator pond, as it is infested with them. In the distance is the illimitable ocean, with its ever varying hues of violet, azure, pale green, white, always reflecting the summer clouds, and rippling with every breeze. Three little coasting schooners are anchored not far from the coast in Black River harbor, and last night I saw the red port light of a vessel far out at sea. If my darlings were only here to enjoy it with me.

But to return to the *"Voyage autour de ma chambre,"* the floor is brown, beautifully polished, as indeed it ought to be, for the Jamaica servants are so lazy, you always have to have two housemaids no matter how small your family, as one always cleans the floors and the other makes the bed. No servant will do anything except what they bargain for. The wall paper of my room is green and Sophy has hung up two little pictures, "The Cooper of Nuremberg", and the "Tearose" she got from the tea company. The furniture is old fashioned mahogany, for you see they took the house furnished. Then dear Sophy has made me such a pretty low dressing table, pink cambric and white muslin, which she keeps covered with fresh flowers in some dainty little china baskets she brought me from London.

The house has a long green verandah in arches, over which hang orange trees, and you can pluck them from the bough with ease. Then in front is a small yard made of cement (it is impossible to have grass near the house the insects are so bad). This cement has however circles cut into it, which are filled with earth and planted with bougainvillea, the purple blossoms of which completely overshadow the little yard. In front of the yard is a barbecue where the pimento and coffee berries are dried, and just in front of that again, is a tank, as Santa Cruz Mts. are so dry, the people here depend entirely on their tanks, for all their water. It is not very good, though of course it is filtered, and so we generally squeeze lime juice in it before drinking it. Limes are the only substitute for lemons which are not procurable here. They are a good deal sourer than lemons, but have rather a raw, greenish taste.

I forgot to say that a barbecue was a large stone inclined plane. Just outside the stone yard Sophy has a little garden, in which the most conspicuous things just now (this being the winter, and not many flowers in bloom) are two beautiful plants of poinsettia, a bush covered over with leaves that seem cut out of crimson velvet, so brilliant are they.

Sophy came in this morning with her hands swelled as if bees had been stinging her. It was that she had been setting out some cuttings and the ants had stung her so. The ants are indeed great nuisances. They are all over one's bed, and some kinds eat clothes terribly.

All round the house is a perfect thicket of oleanders with masses of pink blooms. Then too there is a grove of pimento trees or allspice as we call it. The trees are just like orange trees, only larger, and their stems are whiter than orange trees. They are very beautiful with their smooth dark green pointed leaves and white bunches of blossoms, the seed of which is the allspice of trade. It is bought in the market here, for a mere song and is only known by its Spanish name pimento. Indeed the Evans sent for some allspice to a store in Malvern, and they said they had never heard of it, but they supposed if they mixed all the spices in the store it would be right. And they actually did it.

The cat brought in a horrible looking creature yesterday evening. It was a lizard more than a foot long, of an indescribable greenish black color, and covered with hairs. The tail was jointed and about once and a half as long as my hand, while head was horribly repulsive. The cook Frances said it was a chameleon as it changed color constantly but it must have been the chameleon iguana. This habit of Puff's is peculiarly disagreeable as she has no scruples about what she brings into the bedrooms, she has twice brought in snakes.

A box came from Mr. C. Evans and his wife the other day with New Year's presents for them all here, and among them was a dainty little pair of bedroom slippers trimmed with silver fox fur, to which, as none of the family could get them on, I fell heir. I don't feel so badly about it, as Sophy got in it a pair of red morocco ones. Three days yet before I can possibly hear from my dear ones in Va. and I am getting so anxious. It has rained a little every day since I came up here, but the air is deliciously pure and cool (always in comparison with Kingston) as it is in reality very warm and the heat quite enervates one. They are so good about providing me with oranges, my table always has two or three on it, which I constantly wish I could transfer to Mychunk.

Letter home from Martha Jefferson Trice at Ivor Cottage, Jamaica, Feb 22, 1879

My precious ones,

Yesterday morning while we were sitting at breakfast, Daisy handed me your dear letters. I was so nervous at first I could hardly open them. I was so sorry you had both been so poorly! I know how bad those influenzas are. You did not say whether dear Dab's ears were better. I have been so anxious about him. Mary Minor writes me that they have all been laid up with influenza and she was confined to bed some days with it.

Please tell Miss Russell with my love that her cologne was the greatest comfort to me all through my journey. I have not gotten my trunk yet and will not for another week so the valise was invaluable as I had to bring my things up here in it. To tell the truth, my clean things are at rather a low ebb just now as I have had no washing for nearly a month and am without my trunk.

We left Kingston the day after I wrote to you and I came up here by easy stages. That is to say the first two days were easy as we drove only 13 miles each day, but after that we had nowhere to stay all night so the third day was 40 miles. Still, it was unavoidable so we rested the fourth and then on the fifth came on up here 30 miles more. They put a board from the front seat of the carriage to the back and cushions on it, so I lay on a regular bed all the way. I did not wear any corset so that I was quite comfortable and enjoyed the scenery greatly.

The road was bordered with palm trees, orange groves, sheltering wattled huts with fan palm thatch, cottonwood trees, one mass of different cacti and lianas, in short, scenery very like the little chromo in the dear old parlor at home. It surprised me on my way up to see so many squalid huts, when they have all the advantages of climate, food, etc. and won't take advantage of it. The towns of Old Harbor, Porus, and one or two other villages we passed were really not to be compared with Milton and Keswick would be a gorgeous city to them. They were merely dirty negro cabins and, with the exception of Mrs. Lillie in Kingston, all our landladies were mulattoes.

In Spanish town we stayed in a really handsome house with doors and furniture made of mahogany, black with age, and scrupulously clean and polished, brought from Spain and then again in Mandeville our lodging house was extremely comfortable with bright real silver tea services, dish covers, and massive candlesticks and surrounded by a garden filled with rare flowers and still both were mulattoes. Our night at Old Harbor was on the contrary most horrible. Everything was hot, stuffy, and dirty and we were most charmed to escape.

Dear Mrs. Evans met me with open arms and eyes filled with tears which, she afterwards told me, was because as we drove up, she was not thinking about her at the time, but when she saw me leaning back in the carriage, she thought for a moment it was dear Mother. Sophy, too, paid me the highest compliment I could receive, she said I reminded her constantly in manner and appearance of Margie [Martha's sister].

Dear Sophy has improved more than anybody I ever saw, her gentleness and forbearance with Mr. Evans is beautiful and she interests herself in his affairs so kindly and affectionately. If he writes any more nonsense to you about her not being like a sister to him, don't you believe it for I never saw anyone more unselfish, or who tries harder to do her duty. She has passed through a great deal of trouble since she left Va. and I think it is lovely to see how hard she tries to keep bright and cheerful. I think she is truly pious. Her kindness and affection to me exceeds anything from the time she appears at my bedside with the dose of W'cat Indian bitters till she kisses me goodnight.

A strong tie that unites Sophy to all of us, is her devotion to Mother's memory. She never mentions her without her eyes filling with tears and says no one knows the deep love that sprang up in her heart for her in her illness at Mychunk. She tries hard to conquer her reserve, as I saw in Kingston coming up here, as to me, she is entirely unreserved. I read some aloud to her every day as her eyes are still very weak.

If this letter is very incoherent you can set it down to the fact that she is sitting by me playing the guitar, Mrs. Evans in an armchair by the window stopping me every minute or two to tell me some anecdote or bringing in a flower to show "my sweetest child" as she calls me, or dear old Daisy will bring a pillow for my back, or to ask if I am comfortable. The dear old soul met me just as she did Sophy, kissed me, threw her arms around my neck with "how are you darling." I was really touched. She looks very pale and the climate does not suit her. Having to go out into hot sun about the fowls and housekeeping is very weakening to both Sophy and herself while Mrs. E., who sits in the dark drawing room and reads, enjoys it very much. Mr. Evans has been complaining of the cold for several days and putting on thick things but I find my calicoes very comfortable. The sun outside is intensely hot but we have showers every day which makes it pleasant.

Mrs. E. sent you a plan of the house, I believe, my room is at the end of the long front verandah. I think it is marked in your plan Sophy's room as she gave it up for me. It is a large cool room with a polished brown floor and bed carpet of split matting, an old fashioned mahogany chest of drawers, bed, and high washstand and centre table. Then I have two chairs and a rocking chair and Sophy made me the daintiest dressing table of pink cambric and white muslin, which she keeps covered with lovely fresh flowers all the time. The walls are green paper and now I hope you have some idea of my habitation.

I will tell you how I have hitherto spent my days though I am really going to be more industrious, if I could only get a little strength. At seven in the morning we have tea or coffee with bread and butter in our rooms and I would like so much to get up then but the dear old lady always wanders in in nightgown and curlpapers to have a comfortable chat, you know, Margie, they are sometimes almost interminable, but I like to listen to her as it does delight her so to have an auditor. Do you know I am sometimes afraid your talkative sister will forget how to talk here as Mrs. E. delights so in her anecdotes of old times. As you know, they are sometimes very -- well - and yesterday Sophy and I gave her a real scolding on my account, whereat she simply shook her fat sides and is as bad as ever. I thought I should have to rush from the dinner table yesterday, but she only makes matters worse by saying, before her son, Ah! dear, you know I consider you one of the family. But I don't!!

I see very little of Mr. Evans, he is very much taken up writing letters about a place and goes to sleep every evening. I think his brain has softened a good deal. He makes me furious by calling me Patty but has not said anything disagreeable as yet. He will sit sometimes and look at me steadfastly, which you know is not particularly exhilarating, but as a rule he secludes himself.

Well I will never get through the day. After Mrs. E. leaves my room, I have my bath and then at ten we have breakfast. Afterwards, I am with Mrs. Evans until luncheon at two when amongst other things there are almost always oranges which I fairly long for you to have. After luncheon, Sophy and I generally don wrappers and lie on my bed. I read to her while she works, but often Mrs. E. walks in and ensconces herself in the rocking chair and we keep up a desultory conversation until we slip on our dresses to see the sunset over the sea from the verandah, and directly the sun sets it is entirely dark. At 8 we have dinner and after we go in the drawing room, Sophy plays, Mr. and Mrs. Evans go to sleep, and I sit and think of my darlings, for I know they must be all round the fire in the dining room and if anything happens I can fancy my darling little Luly saying, "I wish Jeff was here," or see Dab writing in his diary and Margie (I hope in my old flowered wrapper) "putting finishing touches to the renowned sleeves of her cashmere."

Do you know I put on mine once in Kingston and it was a perfect bag. I have fallen off 7 pounds since the day I left home. However, I think that must be owing to the abscess I had on the ship. I have not had any symptoms of another which has relieved me of a good deal of uneasiness. Yet still, do you know, I have been here now a week and have only been out of doors once for ten minutes. I am beginning to fear I will just be a good for nothing helpless encumbrance all my life to my darlings for if I stand up five minutes or walk the length of the verandah to the drawing room, I feel pain directly, while if I keep still I am quite well. Well, if the worst comes to the worst, I shall try to emulate Cousin Lizzie Davis who made herself so useful sitting still...

There is the greatest cheating in the post office here. The letters from you are only 5 cents while they charge 12 for everyone from here to Va. Now you know that is simply ruinous so I enclose his in yours. I am also going to put only 8 cents on this and you must be sure to tell me if you have to pay any extra, as we shall prove by that if the post is dishonest.

I enclose you a bit of lace bark and dagger plant. They make wedding bonnets and fans of them. You can have no conception of the enormous prices here, turkey 25 cents a pound, butter 62 cents, crasse calico 12 to 18 cents a yard and a four ounce bottle of glycerine is a dollar and six cents extra for the bottle. Think of that. I never imagined such prices.

I have finished *MacLeod of Dare* and am quite disgusted with it. He becomes quite insane and several chapters are taken up with his ravings. Then he entices her by stratagem into his yacht where he makes her a close prisoner and finally, when they are near the land, a storm comes up. He sends all his crew to the shore while it is still calm and then, with this poor girl still fastened down in the cabin and he patrolling the deck, they go down under the waves in the storm. I think Black must be going mad himself.

Mr. E. lent me another of his to read, *The Three Feathers* or as he called it, "Ve free fevers" in which there is a girl he thinks like me but I think is far more like Margie… Tell John the unbeliever that I am really in Jamaica. I believe he thinks me still on the other side of the ocean, just lying per due. But whenever I think of the two thousand miles between me and home, I realize it very strongly.

Sunday evening.

We went to church this morning. Sophy, Mr. Evans and I to St. Albans six miles off. It was raining hard all night and this morning but we did not get at all wet in the carriage… They have different preachers alternate Sundays and this one is very much disliked so next time I will behold all the elite. It is a large stone church shaped like a cross with the aisle and chancel beautifully inlaid with different woods. One thing that impressed me forcibly was the beautiful behavior of everyone. They all, even children of 3 and 4, followed every word of the service, even reading the epistle and gospel and fairly revelling in the hymns. They were *Ancient and Modern* of which Sophy has given me a copy.

I was excessively amused when the clergyman came in. He was preceded by the beadle, a coal black negro in a black alpaca gown and bearing aloft a polished stick as large as my arm and about 3 feet long. The negroes here, some of them dressed as well as we were, all had their regular pews, but the majority were arrayed in gorgeous colors with large hoops and the most rainbow-like head handkerchiefs, fluttering wildly and feet and legs perfectly bare. The men too with nice suits on and handsome prayer books and neither shoes nor stockings. But what would be a lesson to us was the great attention to the service and sermon, which was a very poor one.

Some old women nearly as old as Granny wore white dresses a little below their knees, bare legs and the inevitable bandana surmounted by a large hat with a band of crepe. They would consider it a disgrace to be seen in a sunbonnet. (As the vows of marriage were read it sounded so funny. An old negro man who lives here walked ever so far today in the pouring rain to stand godfather to somebody.

I'm afraid you'll find my letters as interminable and hard to read as Mr. Evans' but I'll write larger if you'd rather. Give my love to all the servants and tell Granny I shall wait till I get to Va. to choose the legates, there are no neighbors here... If Mrs. E. and her son write and say I am not prudent don't credit it, for I really and truly never took such care of myself in my life. I am so anxious to get really well. *Entre nous*, it is just their undue anxiety for I think she is really quite anxious to produce a match between St. G. and myself, but no thank you. It is fairly pouring out of doors.

Feb 27th 1879. Ivor Cottage

The days have passed so uneventfully since I last wrote, that I have only an account to give of the church we attended last Sunday, St. Albans by name. We drove in quite a heavy rain, six miles, and on the way saw some very fine clumps of Bamboos. They have stems like huge reeds but leaves just like the common river willow.

We passed the cemetery near the church, it was a lonely deserted looking place. They make the tombs here of s tone cemented with clay and on top a flat slab of marble enclosing a square of slate which contains the date of birth and death, I have never seen a text, and only these square flat monuments, never an upright tombstone. The church is a very large cross shaped building of white stone, kept scrupulously clean but very bare looking. The aisle and chancel are inlaid with different woods very artistically indeed, but the pulpit is really the most comical little pepper box with steps to climb into it. But one thing that was really wonderful was the beautiful behavior of the entire congregation. They were all negroes but ourselves, on account of the rain and the preacher is not being very popular. Three families announced their intention of going that Sunday "to see Miss Trice" but fortunately I was spared the embarrassment until next Sunday, when I shall feel a little more at home.

The negroes were dressed as clean as possible but nearly all men and women were without shoes or stockings and with only bandannas on their heads. And still everyone had prayer book and Bible and followed every word of the service, even reading the lessons in a semi audible whisper, with the clergyman. I cannot say much for him, he did not at all fill my idea of a model clergyman. Another one will preach next time, a Mr. Ellis. The beadle was a perfectly black man dressed in a robe made of black alpaca with a tucked yoke, and he first presented himself to my astonished vision walking before Mr. Salt in his white surplice and bearing aloft before him a long, polished sharp-pointed stick. I thought it must be to keep any offending members in order, but it was merely to enhance the dignity of the officiating priest. A queer custom prevails in Jamaica of giving out tickets once every year to all communicants and these they are required to show on every sacramental occasion.

Mr. and Mrs. Lawrence, the nearest neighbors, sent me their cards yesterday evening by Mr. Eubank, a young man who is to marry one of their daughters in about a month. I did not see him, but the Lawrences sent a long message about their carriage being broken and hoping I would call. Of course this etiquette and cards is all very grand and right, but I would much rather have had the young ladies call in an unceremonious manner, than the old people's cards.

I have been making some caps of lace, ribbon and velvet, that dear Sophy gave me. Now a year ago, before these caps were worn, I would have been amused to have read of young people's making caps in any old journal I might have come across. I wonder if future generations may ever see the thoughtless lines I have scribbled here. I should be very careful not to write any hasty uncharitable pages in view of such an occurrence, but I am afraid that is my besetting sin, for no matter how hard I try, and how many resolves I make against it, I constantly find myself saying uncharitable things about people. That is one reason why I wish to make this Journal a record of events, rather than people.

We are to start soon to make a tour of the northern part of the island around Falmouth and Montego Bay, in order for Mr. Evans to see a "pen" of 800 acres called "Wales" which his Mother is anxious for him to buy. It has a very nice Cocoa Walk and exports 1200 cocoanuts annually. I must stop now as I caught such a cold while lying in the hammock last night, that it has made my head ache right much. I got my first letters from my darlings last Friday morning while we were at breakfast. It was such a delight to hear they were well though the dear girls had had bad colds. I sent off quite a budget of mail to Kingston to go by the *Etna* which was advertised to sail today but I saw by yesterday's paper that she had been placed in quarantine on account of some Cubans having small pox in the last port where she had touched. I would not have the girls know it for worlds but there was a good deal of yellow fever in Kingston when I was there, and several cases of small pox, beside which Diptheria was fairly raging. But I trust that the kind Father who protected me on the ocean will still guard me while I am so far from my loved ones, and also give them back to me in safety.

A letter home from Martha Jefferson Trice, Ivor Cottage, Jamaica., March 23, 1879

My own darlings,

Your dear letters came on Friday and as I read them with such delight and enjoyment, I little thought with what a heavy heart I should answer them. Dear Mary Minor, who has never omitted writing to me a single mail, also wrote me, but of course I reserved her letter till the last, and then opened it rather carelessly, as my chief interest was in the home news, but imagine what a shock to have the sad, sad news of dear Aunt Mary Jane's [Mary Jane Terrell Davis] having been taken from us. I could not believe it at first as you said nothing about it, and she said "We were so much saddened by cousin Mary Jane's death. I know none of the particulars, but Cousin Margie will tell you all about it as she has been at Willowby since her death."

I cannot understand, when was it? and how, it must have been very sudden. Poor darling Cousin Lucy, how my heart bleeds for her in her great desolation. I thought after her illness last summer, I would have been somewhat prepared for it, but coming so unexpectedly, it was a terrible shock, I nearly fainted. I shall never forgive myself for not having gone to see her before I left home; I ought to have crawled, and now it is forever too late..

We went to church last Sunday, and a Mr. Ellis preached who is the image of Joe Bronaugh. I felt so sorry for him, poor man, as he is very delicate and in addition to the long services, which you know are very much longer in the English church, there were 140 communicants, and he was perfectly exhausted. The time before when there was communion there were 300 communicants. Of the 140 last Sunday there were only 8 whites. There were 30 or forty whites in the congregation, mostly members of the church, but they left before communion, even the vestrymen. It was extremely touching to see the aged negro men and women, dressed in pure white, going up to the chancel, and spite of the *outre* appearance and astounding costume of some of the younger ones, all idea of being amused would have vanished at the solemnity of their faces. One thing I did not like, as it caused a bustle, was two beadles stood ready and demanded the communion tickets on their way to the altar, and then marshalled them up. Of course I mean the blacks, the whites went up first, and then we waited nearly an hour until all the service was over. I send you the bit I wrote that evening.

Miss Maggie Lawrence was married on Thursday morning at the church. The Evans lent them their carriage driver, and horses, and all the house servants went up to help about the breakfast, so Sophy, Daisy and I cleaned up for them. You see they had lived with the Lawrences before they came here and were very much attached to them. Sophy and I got up by day break and proceeded to make up some bouquets as they had asked us to send up any flowers we could. She made one large one and I made a large and a small one, which last had the great honor of being carried by the bride to church. She had several others, one from the bridegroom but she seized this as soon as she saw it and took it with her. It was tea roses and buds and orange flowers, and the large ones were pink oleanders, white roses and another white feathery flower that is lovely. All three were edged with tropical maidenhair, and made flat like a florist's bouquet and were really beautiful. They sent us word they had never seen flowers so beautifully arranged. Miss Lawrence wore a white silk with natural orange flowers and a veil, and her five bridesmaids were dressed in pale pink silk with trailing sprays of flowers. Unfortunately neither bride nor attendants were at all pretty I hear. It was quite a fashionable wedding with white favors on the postillions, and showers of rice, and slippers in the most approved manner.

I was so grieved to hear of Robt. Thurman's arm turning out such a serious thing, his right arm, too. I am afraid he will never have any more use of it, and he was so active and energetic. Please tell him how truly sorry I am, and how I hope it will not be as bad as they fear.

Poor Theodore, how awful to be so suddenly called into eternity! He was such a good natured boy. I remember how briskly and willingly he brought me that water for the flowers Xmas day. We really seem to be living our lives on the edge of an open grave...

I am watched over with hawk-like eyes by the entire family from morning till night, and am in great danger of being entirely spoiled. Margie, Sophy has given me that elastic India rubber cup for you, she says she brought it thinking you would like it as a memento of your trip to the springs. She will certainly come with me I think if there is money enough for both.

We expect to go to Falmouth the last of this week or the first of next. Mr. Reid is expected up to accompany us. We will not be gone more than a week, and the trip is made especially for Mr. Evans to see a place called Wales which his mother and sister are anxious for him to buy instead of one called Roselle which is double the price and in an unhealthy part of the island. I have such a stylish little black silk velvet bonnet with a long ostrich feather curling over it. It does not at all detract from its beauty in my eyes that it is composed of bits of velvet from a hat of dear Sophy's, on an old bonnet, and that the feather is a made one, or that I was the manufacturer from Sophy's materials. It really is very pretty indeed and I put my jet pin in front. I know it will be becoming to both of you.

Dear Sophy is so kind to me. In my great trouble about Aunt Mary Jane she sat by me, and bathed my head with cologne, and dear Mrs. Evans read nearly a whole book of copied poetry out to me. The dear old lady is very low spirited and has not been at all well for more than a week and as neither of her children are either well or particularly happy I often wish I had either of the two sunbeams that gladden Mychunk to help me make the house bright for them. Sophy I think is brighter, though at times she is very sad and all my efforts will scarcely provoke a smile. There are a great many things as you know that I cannot write, and would not say but to my sisters, and for that reason I have discontinued my journal since I came up here, lest I should write down anything about other peoples' affairs, which I would afterwards regret. I shall take it with me to the North however, and put down anything strange I may see.

We still have a good deal of rain, a shower every evening, and they say it is very cool, but the dress I chiefly wear every night is the old striped muslin over black and I am never too cool in it. I make Sophy dress too and wear flowers, which last I consider a great achievement as when I came she would only wear black or white and neither flowers or ribbons, and now she wears both and rings to boot, whereat her mother greatly rejoices.

I got my trunk up from Black River at last a week or two ago, but before that time I was quite comfortable as they had had my clothes washed, and always have it done now every week... Do you know, glad as I would be to hear from Mildred and Clara, I scarcely know how I could answer their letters, the postage from here is so ruinous. I will only put one stamp on this letter and I am afraid you will have to pay again, but I really cannot help it. I could only get three for love or money, as when the Lawrence's store was broken open the other day, it being the post office as well all the stamps were stolen, and there are none nearer than Kingston. I could not let Cousin Lucy pay so I put two on the letter I wrote her yesterday and have only this one left for you.

You must indeed have had a dreadful time getting from Keswick. It sounds almost strange to hear of the train again, there is only one railroad here 20 miles long and the boxes are very little better than our cattle boxes with just board seats and all open to the weather. Up here silence is universal we never hear a sound or see a face from one week to another. I long for the train sometimes.

The trees in the woods here have such exquisite flowers, which the housemaid Margaret, a very good natured girl, brings us in every day. One is covered with spikes of bloom just like the Scarlet Poker only pale yellow, though there is a scarlet kind also. There are flowers of all colors lavender, red, yellow, white, purple, and every shade and shape.

Sophy and I are going for our first ride tomorrow if I am strong enough. The oleanders have put out innumerable fresh blossoms since the rain and the air is filled with their fragrance. The cows and horses are so fond of them, and crop off all the blossoms as far as they can reach. Somebody sent down a lot of lemons here the other day and Frances said she did not think we would care for them so she gave them all to her pigs…

Everybody in the house is writing for dear life to catch the English mail, which goes out today… Oh my darlings how I long sometimes to see you all. Give love to all the neighbors and to the servants… Dear, dear, love and kisses to each one of you. Luly as to whether my tastes are English or American, I am as I will always be-

Your devoted sister Martha

Ivor Cottage, April 2nd 1879.

Let me see, it has been such a long time since. I last wrote in my journal that I scarcely know how to begin. My home correspondence has absorbed all the news I could think of, and it seemed so stale to write it down twice. I shall describe some of the fruit I have seen however.

First the star apple, a green round ball very like a real apple externally but within much softer and with the seeds like a star round the center from which it takes its name. The part immediately round the seeds is what is eaten, it is scooped out with a spoon, and then too a dish is concocted of star apples, oranges, nutmeg and milk, which is called Matrimony and is considered a great delicacy by the Natives but it has, as most other Jamaica fruits, a sickly, mawkish taste. Then there is the granadilla, which is shaped very like a musk melon, though with a green rind. (The rind of the granadilla sappodilla is used for making pies which are sometimes mistaken for green apples.) It is the fruit of a passion flower very like the one we have in Va. but instead of a delicate blossom, it is much coarser and larger with the outer leaves a dull red and a most unpleasant odor. The seeds of the fruit are eaten and are really quite nice, tasting almost exactly

like the Catawba grape.

Then Benthorn brought us some Tamarinds the other day. They are light brown pods with a hard kernel which is covered with a sour, sweet paste that is used for making cooling drinks. Bananas and pineapples are too well known to need any description. The orange season is over and we cannot procure any at all. It is quite provoking to go driving and see innumerable trees covered with golden oranges and know they are Seville oranges and quite uneatable. The citrons are like exceedingly large oranges but the rind is knotted and lumpy all over. The flowering shrubs in the woods about here are really beautiful, and we have a never failing supply as Margaret the house maid, a good natured girl, brings us in a great many. We made such lovely bouquets to send up to the Lawrences two weeks ago when Miss Maggie Lawrence was married. They were so pretty the bride took one of them to church with her.

I have never seen anything to equal the roses of Jamaica. Mrs. Charles Isaacs, a pretty nice little woman who called on me the other day sent us some flowers several times and the most beautiful roses possible, "Gloire de Dijon, Cloth of Gold" etc. were in the greatest profusion.

Sophy and I went for a ride the other day on Una and Jessie. We were arrayed in our best bib and tucker, and looked quite gorgeous when we started off, but when we returned it was quite a different matter. We had but one idea of the road when we set out which was to keep going up, and when, after scrambling up the mountain with a sheer precipice on one side for an unheard of length of way, we commenced to descend abruptly towards the sea. We got quite bewildered and decided we would let the horses guide us and see if they could find our way. But instead of their returning to Ivor, they calmly proceeded into a little bypath, which after a great deal of twisting and turning brought us up to a cottage made of wattles and thatched with the fan palm. There we were instantly attacked by a couple of ill-conditioned curs, but they were called off from their anticipated meal on us by a mulatto woman who showed us into the right road.

Alas, we had lost so much time in our preambulations that a "cloud no bigger than a man's hand" had risen, and no sooner had we emerged from the path with its tangle of lianas and monkey ropes over head into the high road than we saw we were in for a good wetting. When it does rain here, it does it in earnest and no mistake, each drop is as large as a half crown, and at the rate of about a thousand a second, so in a very short time indeed we did not have one dry thread between us. We rode for our lives. I, who a month ago could scarcely sit up, went off full canter with Sophy just after me, but we were still several miles from home, so by the time we reached here our habits were so saturated and our shoes so filled with water we could with difficulty dismount. We were but little the worse for it however, after a day or two of stiffness.

I have not said anything of the sad news I received about a fortnight ago of the death of my dear Aunt, but it has been and is still a great grief to me.

I was surprised the other Sunday when there was communion to see two beadles demanding tickets from all the blacks before they were allowed to go up to the chancel. Their behavior was most admirable, as quiet and decorous as possible, even tiny scraps of three and four would be an example to some "grown ups" of my acquaintance.

Mrs. Evans and I went out to return the Lawrences' call yesterday evening. I feel remarkably grand sometimes rolling swiftly over these excellent roads and attired in one of the pretty dresses Sophy has supplied me with, though when I am sitting in the lap of luxury in this style I feel rather like an impostor on thinking how often I have roughed it and will again gladly.

We expect to go on a tour round the Island in a few days now. We would have gone more than a week ago, but could not procure the additional horses necessary for the journey as we have to cross some very steep hills

View of the Jamaican interior

and will need 4 horses. Then too we have been detained by waiting for Mr. Reid, a friend of the E's who is to travel with us.

Miss Lawrence seemed a friendly nice sort of girl, she asked me to go riding with them sometimes and I shall if I continue to improve as I have ever since I reached these mountains.

Puff brought in a black snake 4 feet long a week ago, to our great disgust and horror.

I have accomplished several poetical effusions since I came here, one of which with several others I sent to Harper for publication, I do not know with what success as yet.

April 14. Ivor Cottage. Easter Monday.

Here I am sitting out under the cocoanut tree, overlooking the sea, as I wanted to find a quiet place for writing. I started down to the graveyard but there are so many cattle out under the oleanders I am quite afraid to venture. There has been a Mr. Reid staying here for the past week and he and Sophy are just going for a ride. He asked me to go driving with him this morning and I refused and he seems quite angry. I went for a drive with him last Thursday, which when we set off he said would only be ten miles, but we went a wrong road, were out all day and when we got back had been 18 instead of ten.

He told us some curious customs they have here about burying people. The grave is dug and the coffin made as soon as it is decided that the person must die, as all interments have to be in 24- hours after death, so that in hot weather the body is often just wrapped in a sheet and buried. Then the negroes always have a belief that the spirit of the dead is hovering over the earth until the ninth night so until then they mourn and then have a wake which is very like the Irish wakes.

The Moravians in Jamaica have such curious customs at Easter. At 4 o' clock on Easter morning they assemble at their church when there is a solemn prayer and a hymn, after which the minister and congregation march in procession two and two to the burial ground in the centre of which the minister stands and has another prayer, then a sermon and after a final hymn the people disperse to their houses which they reach just at daybreak, in time for the early coffee. Formerly they used to march three times round the cemetery which is always prepared for the ceremony by having all the tombs whitewashed, but that was considered unhealthy, so now the people stand outside, the men on one side and the women on the other while a man stands on either side of the clergyman holding a lamp.

The men and women sit on opposite sides of the church and a woman even hands the collection plate to the women. If any of the children go to sleep in church, they are made to stand up before the clergyman, in sight of all the people, as a punishment.

On Saturday we went for a long drive to Yardley Chase, to see a noted view at a cliff overlooking the sea called Lover's Leap. We tried the new horses Errata and Corvino for the first time as leaders, but Errata kicked so violently we had to take her out and have only one in front. The view was really sublime, the white waves dashing on the shore hundreds of feet below us, and the fan palms overhead. Corning back we were in a good deal of danger once or twice but Mr. Reid is a wonderfully good driver, so we reached Ivor safely at 9 o' clock. It was very dark and coming down a steep incline, the leader shied across the road into a clump of bamboos where he was caught, but Mr. Reid held up the wheelers by sheer strength, so we providentially did not come to grief. He and Mr. Evans set off to Kingston tomorrow and will be gone two weeks and when they return, *(Deo volente)* we will go to the North.

I am so anxious about my home people I don't know what to do, my darling little Luly is exposed to scarlet fever, and it seems so long before I can hear. I am just pining for a sight of their dear faces.

May.

I have heard since that dear Luly is safe and well and that they all are stronger than usual this spring. It is such a relief.

Savanna La Mar, May 8th 1879.

I have not written in my Journal for more than a month, as I was taken very ill the day after I wrote last, and am not yet quite recovered. At last we have set out on our journey after many trials and tribulations before starting. At the last moment Mr. Evans turned rusty and declared he would not go because no dray had been provided for the luggage. We had so few things that one was not at all needed for we had four horses in the large carriage and two in Mr. Reid' s buggy. He finally announced just as we were getting in the carriage that if Mrs. Evans hired a four seated buggy at Black River and sent it back for him, he would condescend to accompany us. This she did at $5.00 a day, and we expect him to arrive in state tonight with his bag.

The day before we came was my 24th birthday and the whole family gave me lovely gifts, among the prettiest was a blue easel album from dear Sophy.

We first had to descend a perpendicular mountain 4 miles long and but for Mr. Reid's wonderfully good driving we should infallibly have come to grief. He drives us four in hand and as the horses are young and exceedingly restive, it is quite risky at times, especially when we were winding around the face of a cliff overhanging the sea, with the parapet broken away. The horses balked at one hill and we were detained nearly two hours but he is very strong and very patient so he finally literally put his shoulder to the wheel and pushed the whole carriage up. I am afraid he strained himself badly, as he has scarcely been able to move since.

At Black River we suddenly came out on the seashore for the first time in my life, for when I crossed it was from the heart of New York to Kingston and I stepped from the vessel to the pier. There were no shells on the beach, the ebb of the tide was not sufficiently strong, and I was greatly disappointed at getting out of the carriage to pick up what was apparently a long brown shell, and proved to be instead a slimy sea snail. On my way back to the carriage I got my feet very wet by a wave which advanced very suddenly. We drove so close to the sea again and again yesterday that our carriage wheels were washed by the tide.

Black River is a small ugly stream which gives its name to the town but what we observed as peculiar was that for a long distance out into the Ocean the Stygian stream retained its inky color, not mingling with the lovely tender green of the sea water. We stopped there several hours, indeed too long as we did not reach this place until twelve at night in consequence. We passed such groves of cocoanut palms with their roots washed by the spray, also mangroves which they call oyster trees as their branches hang over into the sea and the oysters fasten themselves to them. Then past the loveliest little bays and inlets, some of which we had to pass through, much to the disgust of the horses.

We have attracted great attention ever since we started by the grandeur of our cavalcade, as except the Governor, nobody has ever driven four in hand before in Jamaica. Sometimes the leaders did turn round and look at us and they either preferred standing alternately on their fore and hind feet to all four at once, but such vagaries, though sufficiently alarming at the time, added a new pleasure to our arrival whole instead of in a fragmentary state. But jesting aside I am certain we should have had a bad if not a fatal accident yesterday had it not been for Mr. Reid, as we were in great danger several times. One hill it took six men to get the carriage up.

The scenery in the moonlight was perfectly fairy like. When we got here we found the whole town asleep, but by the aid of a stray policeman we obtained some information about lodgings. The clock in the courthouse (rather an imposing building) struck the witching hour of midnight as we entered the town, but fortunately the elves had ended their nightly revels so after trying three lodging houses, we got admission into this one, but as the lodging house keeper is said to be mad, I don't know if he will show it to us. Of course supper was unattainable at such an hour, but we had lunch in our basket so that did not matter.

Our bedroom has Venetian blinds opening into the public room which is entirely of jalousies, and the horror of it was that there was no way of closing our blind and Mr. Reid was just on the other side of it in the public room where he slept on a sofa to protect us from any invasion of the madman. He, poor man, not only had no walls but no door, only an arched opening, so he could not have en joyed it particularly.

We expect to go for a drive this evening and tomorrow on to Lucea Day. If Mr. Evans had not been cantankerous, we would have gone on to Montego Bay. We all are rather knocked-up today, as we came 45 miles yesterday. This is a clean straggling village all one street or rather road as there is never any pavement. There are three churches, and it seems prosperous. It is half a mile from the coast, but no shells are on this part of the shore. Sophy had to fasten our jalousies with two knives and two forks at 3 o' clock in the morning. She had several amusing adventures in which Mrs. E. bore a prominent part.

Montego Bay, 1820s, from A Picturesque Tour of the Island of Jamaica, *by Hakewill, 1875*

Montego Bay. May 12th 1879.

We were very much amused at Savanna la Mar by Mr. Seaton's asking Mrs. Evans when she expected "her youngster" meaning Mr. Evans. He looked astounded when the youngster appeared. The youngster has been throughout a killjoy.

That evening Mr. Reid hired a fine pair of horses and took us for a drive. He has been throughout so very kind and good natured to Sophy and myself. I tremble to think of the money he has spent in shells, boats etc. for us not to mention cocoanuts.

Friday morning we started off to go to Lucea Bay and drove along a beautiful road in splendid style. It is really wonderful how well that man controls those unbroken horses. About midday we reached a little place called Green Island where a Mrs. Watson most kindly allowed us to stop in her house for our lunch and where Mr. Reid laid in a large stock of water cocoanuts. After lunch we drove a mile out of the town to see a fine view from a sugar estate called Houghton Hall. On our way thither, as we were rolling smoothly along the beach, the gray mare kicked so violently without rhyme or reason that she became entangled in the harness and threw herself down. At first we thought she had broken her leg but found she was unhurt.

While the driver Nation was settling the harness again, we got out and discovered a quantity of minute shells on the shore and we presented a most ridiculous tableau squatting in the sand picking them up, Mr. Reid peering through his glasses for the tiny shells. Well, we went on the estate and saw the view which was very lovely, indeed I have never imagined more beautiful scenery than there is in this northern part of the island, a combination of mountain and sea view.

When we got back from Houghton Hall, we bowled along merrily towards Lucea, once having to walk some distance on account of the sea having washed away part of the road. We passed that evening several cocoanut groves of many acres in extent all planted in regular rows. Our road has been bordered with fan palms, cocoanuts, and abbey palms, from which the palm oil is manufactured. I have also seen the croton oil tree which has brilliant red flowers and the arrowroot which is rather like the canna. Mr. Reid also invested in some naseberries which are shaped like a peach, with a skin like the russet pear, and a taste wholly unlike either and not good at all.

We reached Lucea at night, a small place but very pretty surroundings. The leaders were led around by an officious negro too suddenly and we came in contact with the curbstone in consequence. In one half second we were surrounded by at least one hundred negroes all shouting, and gesticulating at the top of their speed. They actually seemed to start out of the earth.

Our accommodations have been peculiar to say the least at Lucea. We could not shut our door, which was rather awkward as Mr. Reid circulates freely at unearthly hours and here, although we have a very nice room with the very loveliest view I ever dreamed of, still all four sides are of glass, so we robe and disrobe in public. Spite of these minor disadvantages and that St. G. has made himself systematically disagreeable ever since we started, we have enjoyed our trip so much. Oh if the dear ones at Mychunk were but with me. Sophy says every few miles, If the dear girls and Dabney were only with us, and Mrs. Evans will say, If we only had Margie and Luly, how pleasant it would be.

At Lucea Mr. Reid fairly made himself perfectly bankrupt with the amount of shells he purchased for us. Early in the morning Saturday we drove to a sugar estate two miles out of the town and went all over the works. It was not in motion as it was Sat. but the manager Mr. Dodd showed us so kindly over it all, it was so interesting. We ate some sugar, a very nice light brown that had been growing in the cane fields the day before, think of that. The hot sugar though was the nicest. Then we went in the distillery and saw the rum in all its stages. It is made of all the refuse of the canes.

We then returned to Lucea to breakfast, and afterwards drove up to a place called Houghton Court to thank the proprietor for the great kindness he had showed us the night before in taking in all 8 of our horses free of charge when he heard Mr. Reid was a sugar planter. It was a lovely place with a broad piazza overrun with stephanotis and pomegranates ripening on the walls.

Mr. Clerk was a charming young bachelor, very good looking and I completely lost my heart to him. He was most delighted to see us and regaled us with pineapples, but we could only stay a short time, and then came on here. In the middle of the day, as we were driving here, we stopped in a grove of cocoanuts on the seashore and laid on the sand and refreshed ourselves with cocoanuts. It was really tropical.

Then we went on and on, winding around the edge of the most rugged cliffs. Oh if I could only paint, the exquisite coloring I have seen in the last few days. This is a most lovely place. The house is on a very high hill and looks down on the harbor filled with shipping, among which is a Spanish vessel from Cuba which is only ninety miles off filled with cattle and with the red and yellow flag of Spain at the masthead. The *Don Juan D'Austria*, which brought over 30 Cuban refugees, who were driven from their homes by the cruelty of the Spanish Government.

They transport cattle here in such a cruel manner. They sling them by the horns invariably, which causes them such horrible suffering that many die very soon from it, and the others suffer all their lives from it. The night we got here Mr. Reid got a pilot boat, *The Perseverance*, belonging to a Mr. Guynair, and took us out for a row on the sea. It was 24 feet long and 8 feet broad. He, Sophy and I and the two boatmen, the steersman and a guitar player composed the crew. The music was so very sweet on the water. Among the other things the man played "Sweet Belle Mahone".

We rowed around all the ships and passed just under the bow of a large man of war, then round the hull of a vessel that had been wrecked on the reef and was being broken up and we were out more than two hours. The southern cross was just over us, it is close to the plough which is inverted in the tropics as well as the dipper. The stars here are beautiful, they seem so near and to stand out from the sky. I always think of Jean Ingelow's lines when we are travelling at night. "A cluster of stars, hangs like fruit in a tree."

Mrs. Evans says when we talk of our journey she always thinks of the Israelites. The oars left long waves of light behind them on the water from the phosphorus. I put my hand over the gunwale and was just drawing it through the water watching the glittering drops of phosphoric water fall from my fingers when the pilot called out "Oh! Miss don't do that I beg, or you will have your hand bitten off by a shark." One was caught here last week 8 (20 crossed out) ft. long, and the whole bay is infested with sharks and barracudas, a smaller but much fiercer kind of shark, for the larger ones will run if a boat comes near them, but the barracudas attack whole boat crews. My hand did not play in the water after that I warrant you.

Early the next morning we went down to the beach, we girls and Mr. Reid, and got a quantity of small shells and he gave us another row. We saw sea urchins and sponges far down in the bottom of the sea and bright blue fish flitting about. I have also seen some pure white and some rose color. The water had the loveliest purple and green shades imaginable.

Then we returned to breakfast. The whole house and yard are overrun with stephanotis and double jessamine and is as fragrant as possible. Three sides of our room are blue glass and we do look so ghastly. Mr. Reid went to church but we were too tired. After dinner we went out driving and got a collection of sea urchins and some very perfect seaweed. Then we went on to a cocoanut grove and drank some of the water, and coming back were caught in a heavy shower. We would have made a good subject for *Punch* with our parasols out of the carriage windows and rugs wrapped around us.

A representative cartoon from Punch, *1856*

After tea Mr. Reid told us some amusing stories of his compatriots, one man in Kingston wanted a wife and wrote to a clergyman in England to procure him one. He got a respectable maidservant, got a medical certificate for her health, and sent her over. When she reached Kingston he met her on the pier and she handed him her letter of recommendation saying, "Here is a bill of exchange on you." He said, "I never yet dishonored a draft and will not this one." That was the extent of the wooing and they were married next day.

We were to have gone out boating next morning but Mr. E. persuaded his mother not to allow us. He told Mr. R. he was bitterly opposed to Sophy and my having this trip at all and did not care whether we enjoyed it or not. We were sitting calmly in the sitting room that evening and several strange lodgers were in adjoining rooms when he walked in and in an excited manner made this startling announcement, "Somebody has put my night dress out on the "ruf" and it is soaking wet, how am I to sleep in it. "

His mother suggested a day shirt but he could not be soothed.

Another grievance that rankled in his breast was that he had only one sheet on his bed and he was so incensed by it that poor Daisy had to give up hers to him and sleep on the mattress. It is only customary in lodging houses to provide one sheet but the rest of us did not mind. But our greatest trouble was that Monday morning he openly insulted Mr. Reid in the public drawing room at Montego Bay. Mr. Reid has certainly the most wonderful power of commanding his temper of anyone I ever saw. He at first said he would not go on farther with us but S and I at last persuaded him to do it as we would really have been in danger of our lives if he had not.

Falmouth. Wednesday - May 14th 1879.

We came here from Montego Bay on Monday and found some beautiful large shells at least a quarter of a mile inland. The house where we stayed was covered with stephanotis and Jamaica Jessamine and Mr. Reid keeps us well supplied with flowers and fruit. He has spared no trouble to make us enjoy ourselves.

We had scarcely reached here before we had a call from Mr. and Mrs. Eubank who asked us to lunch next day. The next morning we went into some shops which are enormously expensive and have very few things, but I was fortunate enough to secure a very handsome copy of Kirke White's poems for Mrs. Evans' birthday.

We saw the gogra nut which grows on the thorny palm and is made into earrings, buttons etc. It rained so in the middle of the day we had to postpone our visit to Potosi until later when we drove out there and were most hospitably received by the young couple. I like the people of this side of the island so much better than the other side, there seems the same difference as between the Southerners and Yankees. One is a collection of sugar planters, the other of shopkeepers.

The Eubanks live in a pretty little cottage with a river over hung with bamboos brawling at the back of the house. Then we drove on to Wales accompanied by Mr. Eubank and went over the houses there. It has a view of a magnificent chain of hills and is very rich. I hope Mr. Evans will get it, it would suit both his mother and then we went to see the prettiest place I have seen in Jamaica. It is a very valuable sugar estate worth more than one hundred thousand dollars owned by an old gentleman named Coy and having the most beautiful and extended view I have ever seen. Indeed I have never seen such scenery as on the northern side of this island.

It is a magnificent house with the hall ninety feet long and inlaid with rare woods. They received us so hospitably, gave us orange wine, and begged us to stay longer in Falmouth and come up to spend the day with them. We met Miss Coy his granddaughter, who is exceedingly pretty and has the most fascinating manners imaginable and - is a mulatto! Think of that! And still she was so kind and civil and so well bred. I did not mind at all shaking hands with her.

We go on to Montego Bay again this evening and expect to stop and see a sugar refinery on our way. The number of large fireflies in the grass rivalled the stars above, they looked quite as large.

Falmouth is a dirty ugly little town, very flat and unlike Montego Bay which is lovely. There is however a very pretty church.

The American steamer comes in today but I shall not hear until I get back to Ivor. I long to hear.

The mosquitoes here are worse than the plague of Egyptian flies, my face looks just as if I had the small pox and indeed my whole body, you could not put the end of your finger on a spot that is not red or purple. My hands are quite stiff from their bites.

Our four in hand has continued to attract attention all the time, we constantly hear people exclaim, "Yah! trabellen a gubbernor tile," and whenever Charles is asked at hotels who we are he tells them, "The colonial secretary, the governor's private secretary and their families." You see we have three vehicles and one with 4 horses. Here the cry arose that we were a travelling circus and it was some time before we could disabuse their minds of that opinion.

Sophy and Mr. Reid have gone for a drive as we do not leave here before three but I am almost knocked up and could not sit up long enough to go. So many of the houses here are made with shingled sides as well as roofs. The roots of the mangrove trees are sometimes 20 and 30 feet high out of the ground in arches, and it is to the roots and not to the branches that the oysters cling. The oysters are very small and black and more like English cockles than oysters. I have seen the sago palm which has finer leaves than the cocoanut and is scarcely as tall. I have seen very few of them here.

Montego Bay, May 15th 1879.

We came here from Falmouth last night having been delayed on the road by the insolent behavior of one of the servants in regard to the horses. The men servants in Jamaica are perfectly outrageous.

We arrived at 12 - very much worn out. I have been rather poorly for a day or two, the stairs are rather more than I can manage.

I was much amused at old Mrs. Watson at Green Island. She is a martyr to Dyspepsia and Sophy presented her with some English biscuits. She devoured them and came in a few minutes later saying, "The stomach is very grateful to you ma' am, I assure you the stomach is most thankful for the biscuits." I could not help thinking of Dickens' Skitzlanders and their stomachs, which were removable at will.

We came back an inland road, with very wild rocky cliffs on either side draped with cacti and ferns. This is certainly a lovely place, not to be mentioned the same day as Falmouth.

A ship with all sails set is gracefully gliding up the bay, and the whole sea is dotted with sloops - schooners and droghers. But for Mr. E.'s constant passions we would enjoy our trip so much.

Ivor cottage May 19th 1879

We spent a day at Montego Bay and Sophy went boating but I was so poorly I could not go. From there we started off on Friday morning and went on 30 miles to New Market which we did not reach until twelve at night, the roads were so dreadful. The road wound all the way around the extreme edge of a mountain and was the most dangerous I have ever travelled over, as there was not a sign of a parapet and a sheer fall of several hundred feet. Mrs. Evans said it was fully as dangerous as the Alps. Once in the night one wheel went over the side of a precipice and Mr. Reid had great difficulty in getting us straight. It was so awfully dark Charles had to lead the front horses for miles. Indeed the last two days we were often only saved by Divine interposition, we were in such danger. We stopped for the night in a place which only was planked up inside for six feet, the rest was in strips like a corn house or cattle car on a train, and such cockroaches. They are as long as one's thumb and have great wings and long curled antennae. We could not sleep for them.

We saw the cabbage palm, it has the stem of the cocoanut and the leaf of the abbey palm, and around each leaf is a strip of bark like a thick corn shuck called cabbage bunkah.

We passed some coolies with scarlet turbans and jackets and perfectly bare legs, only a short white tunic. Then some had the tunic and a square of osnaburgs over the head and but partially concealing the bronze breast and body. Mr. Reid accosted one party with "Ka, ha, ji, " (where are you going?). They salaamed profoundly and answered "Kummor sahib" - (Market, sir).

When we reached the market it was very picturesque indeed. The women with their bright bandannas and dresses of every color and the heaps of bananas, breadfruit etc. formed a very bright picture, and the numbers of swarthy coolies with scarcely any clothes at all added greatly to the effect.

Indeed we have seen a good deal of bronze statuary on our road. (Mrs. Evans said she had not expected to see so much statuary out of Italy, for often we passed great boys perfectly naked.) Some children were quite *in puris naturalibus* and did not seem to mind it at all. One poor little beggar boy in a tattered blue shirt, which did not in the least conceal him, came to us when we stopped for money. He had a dreadfully sore foot, apparently scrofulous. We saw more beggars at Santa Cruz, a little mountain village, than anywhere else. An old man in nothing but his shirt, and without any arms, only his hands joined to the armpit, came to the side of the carriage for alms, as well as the little boy, and when we had satisfied their wants to our great disgust a strapping well-dressed lazy negro man coolly asked for money. We did not gratify him however as he calmly said he did not choose to work.

We stopped for lunch and to escape a sudden shower in a cottage made of wattles and with a fan palm roof, and on the wall to my surprise I saw the pictures of the principal actors in the late murder case in England, Mr. and Mrs. Braso, Mrs. Cox and Dr. Tully. They were from an illustrated news, but I scarcely looked to see them in a hut of bushes.

The day before we had been caught in a shower and gotten very wet, so we did not much relish it a second time. We had great difficulty in reaching here, the horses were quite knocked up, and when we hired fresh ones they refused to pull, so we were quite late in reaching Ivor and then to my great disappointment we found our letters had been sent off to Falmouth and I don't know when I will hear from my dear ones.

The servants had everything so very comfortable for us, even fresh flowers in every room and seemed quite delighted with the presents we brought them. The whole air is heavy with the perfume of the stephanotis and frangipane. The latter is like a single pink or white oleander with a yellow centre and a fragrance like the tuberose. It grows on a tree, but it is not pleasant near a house as it is infested with caterpillars which pervade every room.

The Jamaica robins are so pretty. They are tiny grass green birds with a long bill and crimson throat. The canary birds are coal black with very long tails, as large nearly as a crow but slender. We had some breadfruit this morning, it is when raw like a large green osage orange, and when cooked resembles closely, as some writer about Jamaica once said (a chip). I saw whole orchards of guava trees, they are like small green limes with a cap like an apple. We have had chowchows, which are like cymlins plantains, like a banana in shape and inexpressibly horrid to eat, and naseberries.

There is a tree with large broad green leaves called ramoon which is largely used for feeding horses in the dry parishes, they seem extremely fond of it. The men look so funny on the tiny little donkeys with their feet almost touching the ground. There are such numbers of goats in the lowlands there they are considered a mark of wealth and in the mountains of poverty. I saw whole banks covered with purple tradescantia, and the ferns were wonderfully lovely, just like our rarest greenhouse ferns. Mrs. Evans says the calabash trees always remind her of Friesland chickens, and it is really so as the leaves turn backward. I saw at New Market, enormous trees of crape myrtle, truly the flowers in Jamaica are lovely.

The name by which the negroes as a race are called is Quashee and the coolies Chunee. The negroes everywhere on the road accosted us freely without a semblance of bashfulness "Huddee massa, huddee missis, "good trabellin to you," and some we met said "Bon suite missis." Then they would say "Two pooty buccra missees and one great large missis." We were not spared any remarks on our personal appearance, I assure you.

May 23rd 1879

The Jamaica negroes eat cats and kittens with avidity, and occasionally rats. But they make a great deal of money by catching rats out of the cane pieces. The wages are one shilling, 25 cents, for every dozen and sometimes they will bring in as many as ten dozen a day for rats are the bane of Jamaica. Then unless the "busha" or overseer is very shrewd and having the tails cut off in his presence, has them destroyed, they will take away the vermin and their severed caudal appendages, and with a sharp pointed stick make a hole in the body of the animal, insert the tail, and bring them up to be paid for afresh next day. This fraud was practiced many times before it was discovered.

Rats are the only wild thing to be found in Jamaica. There are neither hares, squirrels, opossums, weasels, nor any of the fauna of North America. They have tried to establish rabbits but the rats destroyed them, and owls to kill the rats but they all died. Very few people have any success with their fowls on that account.

Incendiarism is exceedingly common here, the West Indians tell me, it is very easily performed as all the houses are of wood. I have heard of 3 fires by incendiaries in a radius of five miles in the space of a fortnight.

The servants on the north side of the Island are noted for being much more accommodating and civil than on the Kingston side, indeed Mr. Reid says in his district if a person drops their whip etc. and asks a negro on the road to pick it up, he instantly asks how much he is to be paid before doing it.

The Atlas S. S. Co. has changed its schedule and it has been five weeks since I last heard from my dear ones at home. I have heard indeed in that interval but the letters I received left Mychunk five weeks ago, so I cannot say with what anxiety I am looking for the mail, which I expect today.

June 2nd - Ivor Cottage

The last day of our Journey we went to see Holland, W. E. Gladstone's sugar estate and I wished for Luly, though I must say it was one of the most ill appointed we had seen. It had been more than two weeks since they had finished the crop and they had not cleaned up at all. We nearly slipped up in the liquid sugar all over the floors. They have however a revolving cylinder or rather collection of cylinders which will cure a barrel of sugar in 8 minutes. Then too they had two Persian wheels fitted up with buckets which empty as it revolves just like the pictures one sees of the Nile irrigation only on a larger scale. Holland is in a marsh which is notedly unhealthy and seems not at all well cared for. Mr. Gladstone [four-time British Prime Minister] himself has never visited Jamaica but his son the clergyman has.

We had a soursop the other day, it is like a large green pear shaped cucumber with a soft white inside and is eaten with sugar and nutmeg but is very nauseous. So is the avocado pear which looks like a large brown pear but really owes its size to a stone inside as large as my fist and around that is a layer of what closely resembles rancid mutton suet. It is called midshipman's butter. The stone is used for marking clothes, it is held under the material and the initials pricked in with a pin and never washes out.

Mrs. Lawrence sent us some rose apples. They are as large as a peach with a yellow pink skin and a brown seed within and taste and smell just like a damask rose. It is not unpleasant though rather sickening. I have grown so fond of bananas and when I first came I detested them. The leaf of the banana, when properly dried, resembles closely brown silk, the ribs forming stripes. Sometimes bonnets are made of it.

It has rained almost incessantly since we reached here, it is the regular rainy season. We have not been able to leave the house, and sometimes the fogs are so dense we cannot see beyond the verandah. Indeed it rolls into the rooms like clouds of white smoke and wets everything. Ones shoes are quite blue with mildew in a couple of days, and we have to be constantly wiping our books etc. Pictures too, especially photographs, are faded and spotted immediately in this climate, and as for gloves!!!